traditional British Cooking

traditional British Cooking

simple recipes for classic British food

RYLAND
PETERS
& SMALL
LONDON NEW YORK

First published in the United States in 2007
by Ryland Peters & Small, Inc.
519 Broadway, 5th Floor
New York, NY 10012
www.rylandpeters.com

10 9 8 7 6 5 4 3 2 1

Text © Susannah Blake, Fiona Beckett, Tessa
Bramley, Celia Brooks Brown, Tamsin Burnett-Hall,
Maxine Clark, Linda Collister, Clare Ferguson,
Manisha Gambhir Harkins, Brian Glover, Clare
Gordon-Smith, Kate Habershon, Rachael Anne Hill,
Caroline Marson, Annie Nichols, Louise Pickford,
Sonia Stevenson, Linda Tubby, Laura Washburn,
Lindy Wildsmith, Fran Warde, and Ryland Peters
& Small 2007

Design and photographs
© Ryland Peters & Small 2007

ISBN: 978-1-84597-487-9

Printed and bound in China

Library of Congress Cataloging-in-Publication Data

Traditional British cooking : simple recipes for classic
British food /
author, Susannah Blake ... [et al.].
    p. cm.
  Includes index.
  ISBN 978-1-84597-487-9
  1. Cookery, British. I. Blake, Susannah.
  TX717.T72 2007
  641.5941--dc22
2007024125

Designer Jo Fernandes
Editor Céline Hughes
Picture Research Emily Westlake
Production Gordana Simakovic
Publishing Director Alison Starling

Indexer Sandra Shotter

Notes:
All spoon measurements are level unless
otherwise specified.

Uncooked or partially cooked eggs should not
be served to the very young, the very old or
frail, or to pregnant women.

Testing for set in jam-making:
Before you start making jam, always put a
saucer and 2–3 teaspoons in the refrigerator
to cool. Boil the reduced preserve hard for
5 minutes, then take the pan off the heat and
test for set. Take a teaspoon of the preserve,
put it on the cold saucer in the refrigerator
or freezer and leave for 5 minutes. Push it
with a finger—if it offers resistance or crinkles,
it is ready.

To sterilize preserving jars, wash them in hot,
soapy water and rinse in boiling water. Place in
a large pan, then cover with hot water. With
the saucepan lid on, bring the water to a boil
and continue boiling for 15 minutes. Turn off
the heat, then leave the jars in the hot water
until just before they are to be filled. Sterilize
the lids for 5 minutes, by boiling, or according
to the manufacturer's instructions. Jars should
be filled and sealed while they are still hot.

contents

introduction   **6**

soups, appetizers, and snacks   8

fish   34

poultry and game   56

meat   72

on the side   108

desserts   126

breads   166

teatime   180

preserves   220

index   **236**

credits   **240**

introduction

The British Isles have never been blessed with fine weather but if there has been one positive thing to come out of this, it is the natural British gift for cooking the best comfort food. When a dark evening looms and it's blowing a gale outside, the Brits know how to rustle up a warming casserole, a life-affirming pie, or a mouthwatering crumble to make them glad to be in out of the cold.

Years of humble dishes cobbled together from leftovers and pantry essentials, and designed to satisfy a big appetite have brought us time-honored favorites, such as Lancashire hotpot, cottage pie, Yorkshire puddings, and cock-a-leekie. All these, alongside classic trifle, lemon curd, syllabub, and bread and butter pudding, are coming to the fore again and becoming popular dishes in homes and restaurants around the world.

Traditional British Cooking brings you all these and plenty more British-inspired gems. The recipes here will encourage you to make the most of seasonal produce—to celebrate summer with a berry-packed summer pudding and see in the fall with blackberry cranachan. There is also much to learn about the myriad regional dishes on offer—Scottish shortbread, Welsh speckled teabread, Irish soda bread, and Yorkshire cheesecake, to name but a few.

Finally, if there's one occasion that epitomizes the British culinary tradition, it's the inimitable afternoon tea. With a whole chapter dedicated to this noble tradition, your British cooking repertoire will be complete.

Dip into this indipensable book and discover what easy, hearty, and delicious recipes British cooking has to offer.

soups, appetizers, and snacks

Watercress has fresh crunch and a subtle peppery taste—a real palate cleanser. Buy it in bunches, with long stems, an abundance of flawless dark green leaves, and a clean fresh smell. Store in the refrigerator, wrapped in damp newspaper or paper towels, for up to 2 days.

watercress soup

2 tablespoons olive oil

1 onion, chopped

1 leek, chopped

2 large potatoes, chopped

2 teaspoons all-purpose flour

6 cups chicken or vegetable stock

10 oz watercress, stalks removed and leaves chopped

a bunch of fresh flatleaf parsley, chopped

sea salt and freshly ground black pepper

serves 8

Heat the olive oil in a large saucepan and add the onion, leek, and potatoes. Cook for 15 minutes, or until soft and translucent.

Add the flour, mix well, then add the stock and a little seasoning. Heat to simmering and cook for 30 minutes. Using a stick blender, process until smooth.

Add the watercress and parsley and simmer for 5 minutes. Season to taste, then serve.

This is a gorgeously smooth and velvety soup that will suit all tastes and any occasion, from picnics to dinner parties. To ensure a really smooth texture, it is very important to blend, then strain the soup before serving hot or chilled.

leek and potato soup
with watercress purée

5½ tablespoons unsalted butter

2 onions, finely chopped

1 lb leeks (white part only), finely chopped

1 potato, chopped

5½ cups chicken stock

1¼ cups milk

⅔ cup sour cream or crème fraîche, plus extra to serve

sea salt and freshly ground white pepper

watercress purée

1 cup watercress, stalks removed

⅓ cup extra virgin olive oil

serves 6

To make the watercress purée, put the watercress leaves in a blender with the olive oil. Blend until smooth. Pour into a screwtop jar and set aside until needed.

To make the soup, melt the butter in a large saucepan and add the onions and leeks. Stir well, add 3 tablespoons water, cover tightly, and cook over gentle heat for 10 minutes, or until soft and golden, but not at all brown.

Stir in the potatoes and chicken stock. Bring to a boil, reduce the heat, cover, and simmer for 20 minutes, or until the potato is tender. Stir in the milk, then purée in a blender or with a stick blender. Press the purée through a strainer, then return it to the pan. Stir in the sour cream and season. Let cool and chill (if serving chilled, add extra seasoning) or serve hot in warm soup bowls with a swirl of watercress purée and spoonful of chilled crème fraîche.

A few dried porcini will give a stronger flavor to a soup made with regular cultivated mushrooms. Use large portobellos to give a deeper color as well as flavor.

cream of mushroom soup

1 oz dried porcini mushrooms

¼ cup olive oil

6 large portobello mushrooms, wiped, trimmed, and sliced

1 onion, finely chopped

3 garlic cloves, peeled and crushed

a pinch of freshly grated nutmeg

leaves from a large bunch of fresh parsley, finely chopped

5 cups boiling chicken or vegetable stock

4 tablespoons butter

¼ cup all-purpose flour

sea salt and freshly ground black pepper

to serve

4–6 tablespoons coarsely chopped fresh parsley

4–6 tablespoons sour cream or crème fraîche

serves 4–6

Put the dried porcini in a bowl, add 1 cup boiling water and let soak for at least 15 minutes. Heat the olive oil in a skillet, add the portobello mushrooms, and sauté until colored but still firm. Reserve a few slices.

Add the onion to the skillet and sauté until softened, then add the garlic, nutmeg, and parsley. Rinse any grit out of the porcini and strain their soaking liquid several times through cheesecloth or a tea strainer. Add the liquid and the porcini to the skillet. Bring to a boil, then transfer to a food processor. Add 2 ladles of the boiling stock, then pulse until creamy but still chunky.

Heat the butter in a saucepan, stir in the flour and cook gently, stirring constantly, until the mixture is very dark brown (take care or it will burn). Add the remaining stock, 1 ladle at a time, stirring well after each addition. Add the mushroom mixture, bring to a boil, then simmer for 20 minutes. Season to taste, then serve topped with the reserved mushrooms, parsley, and a spoonful of sour cream.

note If you use a blender to make soup, the purée will be very smooth. If you use a food processor, it will be less smooth, and if you use the pulse button, you can make the mixture quite chunky.

One of the great classics of the soup world is pea and ham soup—a comforting, warming winter soup. This is a modern version using fresh or frozen peas and readily available bacon.

fresh pea soup
with mint and crispy bacon

1 tablespoon olive oil

4–8 slices of very thinly cut fatty bacon

1½ cups shelled green peas, fresh or frozen

1 quart boiling ham or chicken stock, or water

sea salt and freshly ground black pepper

4 tablespoons light cream, to serve

serves 4

Heat the olive oil in a skillet, add the bacon, and sauté until crisp. Remove and drain on crumpled paper towels, or drape over a wooden spoon so it curls.

To cook the peas, microwave on HIGH for 3–4 minutes, or follow the package instructions. Alternatively, simmer in boiling water with a pinch of salt for 2–3 minutes or until tender. Drain.

Put the peas in a blender with 1–2 ladles of the boiling stock. Blend to a purée, adding extra stock if necessary. Add the remaining stock and blend again. Taste and adjust the seasoning. Reheat, thinning with a little boiling water if necessary, then ladle into heated soup bowls and serve, topped with the crispy bacon and a swirl of cream.

variation Cook the peas, drain, and let cool, then put in the blender with 8 ice cubes and enough water to make the blades run. Blend to a purée, then thin with ice water to the consistency you like. Season to taste and serve topped with sliced scallions.

1½ tablespoons butter

1 onion or 4 shallots, sliced

1 cup grated Cheddar cheese

⅓ cup ale or lager

1 teaspoon mustard

a pinch of sea salt

2 eggs, lightly beaten

4 slices of bread

freshly ground black pepper

serves 2–4

Welsh rabbit—also known as rarebit—is a glorified version of cheese on toast. It dates back to the mid-sixteenth century, but over time has evolved into countless variations. If you need a comforting snack, this easy-to-make version is hard to beat.

welsh rabbit

Melt the butter in a heavy-based saucepan, add the onion, and cook until it has softened. Add the Cheddar cheese, ale, mustard, and salt. Stir over low heat until the cheese has melted.

Add the eggs and stir until the mixture has thickened slightly, about 2–3 minutes. Don't overcook or you will end up with scrambled eggs.

Toast the bread on both sides, then spoon the cheese mixture onto the toast and cook under a hot broiler, until puffed and gold-flecked. Serve with lots of black pepper.

Homemade sausage rolls are relatively quick and easy to make, and they are delicious served warm from the oven. These snack-size sausage rolls are ideal for gatherings with family and friends over the Holiday season.

sausage rolls

1 lb chilled fresh ready-made puff pastry dough

1 lb pork sausage meat

flour, to dust

milk or beaten egg, to glaze

makes about 40 sausage rolls

Preheat the oven to 425°F.

Remove the dough from the refrigerator about 20 minutes before using. Cut the block of dough in half. Roll out one piece on a lightly floured surface to form a rectangle about 16 x 8 inches. Cut the dough rectangle in half lengthwise to form 2 equal-size strips.

Divide the sausage meat into 4 equal pieces. On a lightly floured surface, roll out 2 of the sausage-meat portions into long rolls, each the length of the dough strips.

Lay a sausage-meat roll lengthwise on each strip of dough. Brush the dough edges with a little water, then fold one side of the dough over the sausage meat and press the long edges together to seal using the tines of a fork—this will also add a decorative edge to the sausage rolls.

Repeat with the remaining dough and sausage meat. Trim the ends of each long roll. Lightly brush the dough all over with milk to glaze, then cut each long roll into 1¾-inch lengths. Using a sharp knife, make a slit in the top of each sausage roll.

Transfer the sausage rolls to 2 baking sheets, leaving a space between each one. Bake for 15 minutes, then reduce the oven temperature to 350°F, and bake for a further 10–15 minutes, or until the sausage rolls are deep golden, crisp, and cooked. Transfer to a wire rack to cool and serve warm or cold.

What could be more British than creamy, crumbly Stilton, the king of English cheese? The combination of pear and Stilton in this appetizer works wonderfully, both visually and on the tastebuds.

sweet pear and stilton melt

4 firm, ripe pears, halved lengthwise and cored

2 tablespoons freshly squeezed orange juice

2½ oz Stilton cheese, crumbled

1 tablespoon dried cranberries or golden raisins

1 tablespoon toasted chopped hazelnuts

2 teaspoons finely grated unwaxed orange peel

1 tablespoon extra virgin olive oil

4 handfuls of bitter salad leaves

sea salt and freshly ground black pepper

serves 4

Preheat the broiler to medium-hot and line the broiler pan with aluminum foil.

Brush the pear halves with a little orange juice. Put the Stilton in a bowl and beat with a wooden spoon until creamy. Stir in the cranberries, hazelnuts, orange peel, and enough orange juice to moisten. Fill the pear hollows with the cheese mixture.

Transfer the pears to the broiler tray and broil for 3–4 minutes, or until the cheese just begins to melt. Remove from the heat.

Put the olive oil, remaining orange juice, and seasoning to taste, in a large bowl. Beat well. Add the salad leaves and toss to coat. Divide the salad leaves between 4 serving plates. Put 2 pear halves on each plate and serve immediately.

variation Leave the pears whole. Core them with an apple corer and brush with lemon juice to prevent discoloration. Make the filling as above and use to stuff the pears, filling from the base. Chill for at least 30 minutes, then serve on the dressed salad leaves.

Treated properly, parsley, garlic, and extra virgin olive oil can create a superb, vividly scented green oil which will make any seafood taste good. Drizzled over scallops, which have been briefly marinated in lemon juice and lovely olive oil, it becomes a sensational recipe.

char-grilled scallops
with parsley oil

2 garlic cloves, peeled and crushed

¼ cup extra virgin olive oil

freshly squeezed juice of 1 lemon

1½ cups plump fresh sea scallops, about 16

a small handful of fresh chives (optional), to serve

parsley oil

a small bunch of fresh parsley, finely chopped, ¼ cup

½ cup extra virgin olive oil

1 garlic clove, peeled and crushed

sea salt and freshly ground black pepper

8 short wooden skewers or satay sticks, soaked in water for 30 minutes

serves 4

Mix the garlic, olive oil, and lemon juice in a shallow, nonmetal dish. Pat the scallops dry with paper towels. Make shallow criss-cross cuts in each one. Prick the corals with a toothpick to prevent splitting. Add the scallops to the dish of marinade, turning once, and set aside while you prepare the parsley oil.

To make the parsley oil, put the parsley, olive oil, and garlic in a blender and blend until smooth. Strain into a bowl or just pour straight from the blender and use this vivid green oil as both garnish and condiment.

Drain the scallops, then thread 2 onto each skewer. Pour the marinade into a skillet, bring to a boil, and cook until reduced to a sticky golden glaze. Add the scallops and sizzle them in the glaze for 1 minute on each side (or a little longer if preferred). Serve drizzled with parsley oil and a separate small dish of oil for dipping. Sprinkle with seasoning and decorate with a bundle of chives, if using.

note Always try to buy unsoaked or "dry" scallops. Do not buy any that are sitting in water. The water soaks into the flesh and when the scallops hit the pan, the water seeps out and makes the scallops mushy.

The salty, smoky taste of salmon blends well with the starchy texture of potatoes. Fava beans are one of the few foods that don't seem to suffer from the freezing process. In fact, since they're frozen almost as soon as they're picked, their texture can often be better than those you buy at the market. Like most green vegetables, fava beans are very good cooked in a microwave.

smoked salmon salad

Microwave the fava beans on HIGH for 3 minutes if fresh, or 2 minutes if frozen. Transfer immediately to a bowl of ice water. When cold, pop them out of their grey skins, discard the skins, and reserve the beans.

Boil the potatoes whole, in their skins, until tender, about 15–20 minutes (the time depends on the size of the potatoes). Drain, then toss in 2–3 teaspoons of the olive oil (gently so as not to break the skins). Cut the potatoes in half and arrange on 4 chilled plates. Top with the fava beans and smoked salmon. Sprinkle with seasoning and the chives. Drizzle with about 1 tablespoon olive oil per plate and sprinkle with 1 teaspoon cider vinegar.

2 cups shelled fava beans, fresh or frozen

12 red new potatoes

4–5 tablespoons extra virgin olive oil

4 oz smoked salmon, diced

a handful of fresh chives, snipped

4 teaspoons cider vinegar, white wine vinegar, or rice vinegar

sea salt and freshly ground black pepper

serves 4

The freshest, crispest green vegetables, like peas, beans, zucchini, asparagus, and their kin, bought in season when they are at their peak, make a fantastic, satisfying salad. They marry particularly well with the milder members of the onion family—pearl onions, baby scallions, or red onion.

green vegetable salad
with hazelnut dressing

about 12 mini asparagus tips

a handful of thin green beans (untrimmed)

4 baby zucchini, cut into thirds lengthwise (optional)

4 oz sugar snap peas

4 oz shelled green peas

4–6 very thin scallions

hazelnut oil, to drizzle

3 oz hazelnuts, pan-toasted in a dry skillet, then lightly crushed into halves or big pieces

sea salt and freshly ground black pepper

fresh Parmesan cheese, to serve

hazelnut dressing

6 parts extra virgin olive oil

1 part white wine vinegar

½ teaspoon mustard

serves 4

Microwave the asparagus tips, beans, zucchini, sugar snaps, and green peas separately, on HIGH, for 2 minutes each, then transfer immediately to a bowl of ice water. Alternatively, bring a large saucepan of water to a boil, then add each vegetable and blanch until just tender, but still al dente. Keep the peas until the end, and drain well before chilling.

To make the hazelnut dressing, put the olive oil, vinegar, mustard, and seasoning in a salad bowl and beat well with a fork or small whisk to form an emulsion. Put in a bowl, add the drained vegetables, and toss until lightly coated. Arrange the vegetables on a serving platter or 4 salad plates, then drizzle with hazelnut oil and top with toasted hazelnuts. Shave fresh Parmesan over the top and finish with seasoning, to taste.

note Nut oils and nuts become rancid very quickly, so buy them in small quantities. Use them quickly, keep them sealed, and store in the refrigerator, returning to room temperature for serving.

A splendid summery take on roast beef—perfect as a special-occasion salad for a summer lunch party. For the best flavor, let the meat return to room temperature first. Don't salt it first, or you'll draw out the juices. Serve with beef's ideal accompaniment—finest homemade Horseradish Sauce (page 125).

rare beef salad
with watercress

olive oil, to grease

1 lb beef tenderloin, about 20 inches long, well trimmed

1 lb watercress or other peppery leaves, such as arugula, or wild garlic (ramps)

Horseradish Sauce (page 125), to serve

sea salt and freshly ground black pepper

serves 8

Preheat the oven to 400°F.

Brush a heavy-based roasting pan with olive oil and heat on top of the stove until very hot. Add the beef and seal on all sides until nicely brown. Transfer to the oven and roast for 20 minutes. Remove from the oven and set aside to fix the juices. Season.

Let the meat cool to room temperature and reserve any cooking juices. If preparing in advance, wrap closely in aluminum foil and chill, but return it to room temperature before serving.

Arrange the leaves down the middle of a rectangular or oval serving dish. Slice the beef into ½-inch thick slices with a very sharp carving knife (or an electric knife). Arrange in overlapping slices on top of the leaves and pour over any cooking juices from the roasting pan or carving board.

Serve with Horseradish Sauce.

This salad makes a wonderful appetizer or dinner dish. Be careful not to overcook the chicken livers, or they will become dry and tough, instead of perfectly cooked, juicy, and soft. Chicken livers are available in butcher's shops and large supermarkets, fresh or frozen.

chicken liver salad

4 slices of toasted or fried bread

8 oz mixed lettuce leaves

8 oz chicken livers

4 tablespoons butter

2 tablespoons olive oil

½ cup red wine

sea salt and freshly ground black pepper

serves 4

Put the toast on 4 small salad plates and top with the lettuce leaves.

Trim the chicken livers, removing any tubes and any dark or slightly green patches. Cut the livers into equal pieces.

Melt the butter and olive oil in a large saucepan. When really hot, add the chicken livers and cook for 2 minutes on one side, then turn them over and cook for 2 minutes more.

Season, then carefully remove the livers from the saucepan, using a slotted spoon, and divide them between the plates, laying them on top of the lettuce leaves.

Add the wine to the pan juices and bring to a boil, stirring. Boil hard for 1 minute, then pour the hot dressing over the livers and serve.

fish

Nothing beats a steaming, creamy fish pie on a cold winter's evening. The mustard and boiled eggs lift this from a safe dinner dish to a fantastic winner of a pie.

traditional fish pie

Preheat the oven to 400°F.

Put the milk in a wide saucepan, heat just to boiling point, then add the fish. Turn off the heat and let the fish poach until opaque—do not allow to overcook.

Meanwhile, melt 1¼ sticks of the butter in another saucepan, then stir in the mustard and flour. Remove from the heat and strain the poaching liquid into the pan.

Arrange the fish and eggs in a shallow pie dish or casserole dish.

Return the pan to the heat and, whisking vigorously to smooth out any lumps, bring the mixture to a boil. Season to taste. (Take care: if you are using smoked fish, it may be salty enough.) Pour the sauce into the casserole dish and mix carefully with the fish and eggs.

Cook the potatoes in boiling salted water until soft, then drain. Return to the pan. Melt the remaining butter in a small saucepan. Reserve 4 tablespoons of this butter and stir the remainder into the potatoes. Mash well and season. Spoon the mixture carefully over the sauced fish, brush with the reserved butter, and transfer to the oven. Cook for 20 minutes, or until nicely brown.

note If you can't find smoked haddock, you can sprinkle 4 oz smoked salmon, finely sliced, over the poached fresh haddock just before adding the sauce.

2 cups milk

1½ lb Finnan or fresh haddock, skinned

2¾ sticks unsalted butter

1 tablespoon English mustard powder

¼ cup all-purpose flour

2 hard-cooked eggs, peeled and quartered

2 lb baking potatoes

sea salt and freshly ground black pepper

serves 4

This classic Anglo-Indian recipe began life in colonial India as a breakfast dish, but nowadays it is great whatever time of day you choose to make it.

kedgeree

1 lb undyed smoked haddock fillets

2 bay leaves

1 cup basmati rice

3 tablespoons olive oil

5 scallions, finely chopped

1–2 garlic cloves, peeled and finely chopped

1–1½ tablespoons curry powder

freshly squeezed juice of 1 lemon

2 hard-cooked eggs

2 tablespoons chopped cilantro

freshly ground black pepper

lemon wedges, to serve

serves 4

Put the haddock, bay leaves, and ½ cup water in a sauté pan and bring to a boil. Cover, reduce the heat, and simmer for 5 minutes. Remove the pan from the heat, drain, and, when cool enough to handle, peel the skin off the fish and flake the flesh with a fork. Set aside.

Meanwhile, bring a large saucepan of water to a boil. Add the rice and return to a boil. Stir, then reduce the heat and simmer for 10 minutes, until the rice is cooked but still has a slight bite to it. Drain and reserve.

Heat a large, nonstick sauté pan. Add the oil, scallions, and garlic and fry gently until softened and slightly colored, about 6 minutes. Add the curry powder and cook for 2 minutes. Add the lemon juice, the reserved haddock, and rice. Cut one egg into wedges and reserve. Chop the other one into small pieces and add to the pan. Sprinkle with the cilantro and season to taste with pepper. Continue to heat, stirring gently, until piping hot.

Transfer the kedgeree to a warm serving dish. Top with the egg and lemon wedges and serve immediately.

variation Use 14 oz fresh salmon fillets instead of the haddock and cook as above. Alternatively, add 2½ oz smoked salmon, cut into thin strips, at the same time as the chopped egg.

1/3 cup olive oil

3 garlic cloves, peeled and chopped

2 onions, chopped

2 leeks, trimmed and sliced

3 celery stalks, sliced

1 fennel bulb, trimmed and sliced

1 tablespoon all-purpose flour

1 bay leaf

a sprig of fresh thyme

a generous pinch of saffron threads

three cans chopped tomatoes, about 6 cups

2 quarts fish stock

2 lb monkfish tail, cut into 8 pieces

1 lb mussels in shells, scrubbed

8 scallops

8 uncooked shrimp, shell on

a bunch of fresh flatleaf parsley, chopped

sea salt and freshly ground black pepper

serves 8

Make this on a summer's day for a taste of the seaside. Don't forget to provide a few empty dishes for discarded shells and some bowls of warm water with lemon slices for washing fingers.

easy fish stew

Heat the oil in a large saucepan and add the garlic, onions, leeks, celery, and fennel. Cook over low to medium heat for 10 minutes until soft.

Sprinkle in the flour and stir well. Add the bay leaf, thyme, saffron, tomatoes, and fish stock, and season to taste. Bring to a boil, then simmer for 25 minutes.

Add the monkfish, mussels, scallops, and shrimp, cover with a lid, and simmer very gently for 6 minutes. Remove from the heat and set aside, with the lid on, for 4 minutes. Add the parsley and serve with plenty of warm crusty bread.

This traditional Scottish stew—known as Cullen Skink—is made with smoked Finnan haddock, thickened with potatoes, and enriched with a splash of cream. If you can't get this fish, use another naturally smoked haddock instead—but not the artificially dyed variety!

smoked haddock stew
with potatoes and celery root

2 tablespoons unsalted butter

2 onions, finely chopped

2 potatoes, diced

1 celery root, about 1 lb, finely chopped

1 cup fish stock

2 cups hot milk

2 lb undyed smoked haddock, preferably Finnan

about ⅔ cup heavy cream

a large handful of fresh parsley, chopped, to serve

sea salt and freshly ground black pepper

serves 4

Preheat the oven to 300°F.

Heat the butter in a large saucepan, add the onions, potatoes, and celery root, and cook, stirring until softened. Add the fish stock, 1 cup water, and the pepper. Bring to a boil, then pour into a casserole dish.

Cover and cook in the preheated oven for 50 minutes, or until the potatoes and celery root have disintegrated into the liquid and the mixture has thickened. Remove from the oven.

Pour the milk into the casserole. Put the smoked haddock, skin-side up, on top of the vegetables and return to the oven for a further 4–5 minutes, or until the fish is cooked. Remove from the oven and take out the haddock. Peel off and discard the skin and bones. Flake the fish with a fork and set aside.

Stir the cream into the casserole and reheat. Return the fish to the casserole, then serve in deep dishes with the chopped parsley.

variation For a smoother soup-stew, after removing the fish from the casserole, press the remaining mixture through a coarse strainer. Proceed with the recipe and add extra milk or cream, if necessary.

Celery leaf is a delicious herb, and plants are now available in pots from garden centers. You could also use the pale leaves growing inside an ordinary head of celery. Celery and flatleaf parsley leaves are perfect crisply fried and curly parsley is also good. Chervil and parsley are used to flavor the coating on the fish.

crisp-fried herbed halibut
with shoestring potatoes

1½ lb salad potatoes

peanut or safflower oil, for deep-frying

1 egg white

1 tablespoon milk

1½ lb halibut fillet, cut into 8 pieces

3 sprigs of fresh chervil

3 sprigs of fresh flatleaf parsley

⅔ cup all-purpose flour

1 teaspoon black sesame seeds

½ teaspoon chile powder

sea salt and freshly ground white pepper

an electric deep-fryer

serves 4

Using a mandolin, cut the potatoes as thinly as possible into strips, then put into a bowl of cold water to rinse off the starch. Drain and dry well with paper towels.

Fill a deep-fryer with oil to the manufacturer's recommended level and heat to 350°F. Working in batches, fry the potatoes until golden, then drain on paper towels. Keep hot.

Put the egg white and milk in a bowl and mix. Rub the fish with the egg white mixture. Finely chop the leaves from the chervil and parsley.

Sift the flour into a bowl, then add the chopped chervil and parsley, the sesame seeds, chile powder, and seasoning.

Deep-fry the celery and parsley leaves. Be careful, they spit furiously, but will be crisp as soon as the spitting stops. Remove and drain on paper towels. Dip the fish into the bowl of flour mixture to coat, and fry 2 pieces at a time for 2–3 minutes until just cooked. Drain on paper towels and serve with the fried leaves and crisp shoestring potatoes.

This recipe calls for a large piece of cod, the middle cut, known as the saddle. You may have to ask your fish seller to cut it specially. Save up this recipe for a special meal—it's terribly easy to throw together but looks and tastes impressive.

½ cup bread crumbs

½ cup fresh flatleaf parsley, chopped

⅓ cup hazelnuts, crushed

2 lb saddle of cod

sea salt and freshly ground black pepper

mustard mash

2 lb floury potatoes

2 teaspoons English mustard powder, mixed to a paste with 1 tablespoon water

4 tablespoons unsalted butter

hot milk

serves 4

roast cod
with mustard mash

Preheat the oven to 400°F.

Combine the bread crumbs, parsley, and hazelnuts. Put the fish in a roasting pan and press the crumb mixture over the top. Cook in the preheated oven for 25–35 minutes, or until the fish turns milky-white.

To make the mustard mash, cook the potatoes in a pan of boiling salted water until soft and tender. Drain and mash well, stir in the mustard and butter, then beat in enough milk to produce the consistency you prefer.

Serve the cod with the mustard mash and a sprig of parsley.

4 fresh trout fillets
(each weighing about 5 oz)

1 tablespoon olive oil

5 tablespoons unsalted butter

freshly squeezed juice of 1 lemon

1 tablespoon small capers,
drained and rinsed

1 tablespoon grainy mustard

a bunch of fresh tarragon,
chopped

sea salt and freshly ground
black pepper

pan-fried potatoes

2 lb new potatoes, scrubbed
and halved if large

2 tablespoons olive oil

1½ tablespoons unsalted butter
(optional)

2 garlic cloves, peeled
and thinly sliced

braised peas and lettuce

2 tablespoons unsalted butter

1 onion, finely chopped

2 tablespoons white wine

3 tablespoons crème fraîche

1⅔ cups frozen petits pois

1 small romaine lettuce, shredded

serves 4

All the elements of this meal combine wonderfully to make a satisfying weekday dinner. It may seem like there is a lot to prepare but it is really quite easy and the secret is in the timing.

broiled rainbow trout fillets
with mustard and caper butter

To make the pan-fried potatoes, cook the potatoes in a large pan of boiling salted water for about 10 minutes, or until they are just tender. Drain well. Heat the oil with the butter (if using; it gives the potatoes a better flavor) in a large skillet and add the hot potatoes. Sauté them over medium heat, turning frequently until they are evenly golden brown, about 10–15 minutes. Toss the garlic in for the last 2 minutes of cooking. Drain on paper towels, season with salt, and serve while hot and crispy.

Lay the fish on a lightly-oiled broiler pan, skin-side down. Drizzle with the olive oil and season.

Melt the butter in a small saucepan over low heat and add the lemon juice, capers, and mustard. Mix to combine and set aside.

To make the braised peas and lettuce, melt the butter in a pan and cook the onion for 2–3 minutes until softened but not colored. Add the white wine and let bubble until the liquid has evaporated. Add the crème fraîche and seasoning. Add the peas and lettuce, and cook for 2–3 minutes until the peas are tender and the lettuce has wilted.

Place the fish under a medium-hot broiler for about 4 minutes. Carefully remove from the broiler pan and arrange on warmed plates. Add the chopped tarragon to the butter sauce (at the last moment so that it keeps its vibrant green color) and immediately pour over the trout.

Originally a way to cook fresh trout brought straight from river to fire, this method lends itself beautifully to cooking a whole fish so that it retains all its flavor and moisture. It looks fantastic and couldn't be simpler!

salmon baked in newspaper

1 fresh salmon, about 3 lb, gutted but not scaled

1 unwaxed lemon, sliced

a bunch of fresh herbs, such as dill, tarragon, chervil, and bay leaves

4 sheets of uncolored newspaper

serves 6

Preheat the oven to 400°F.

Open the newspaper sheets and arrange one on top of each other. Fill a sink with cold water and soak the newspaper in it. Wet a large sheet of waxed paper and open it out flat on a work surface.

Put the salmon on top of the waxed paper and tuck the lemon slices and herbs into the cavity. Wrap up in the waxed paper. Spread the soaked newspaper on the table and put the wrapped fish at the long edge. Roll up, tucking in the sides. Put the fish on a baking sheet and bake for about 45 minutes.

Remove from the oven and unwrap. Test to see if the fish is cooked through (the eye should be white and the flesh opaque to the bone). If not done, wrap up again, spray with water, and cook for a further 10 minutes and check after that.

To serve, unwrap the fish and roll onto a serving platter in all its glory. It will taste sublime.

These fish cakes freeze well, so are useful for get-ahead weekends. Any type of fish can be used.

traditional fish cakes

2 lb potatoes, peeled

3 tablespoons butter

¼ cup milk

1 lb salmon, cod, or halibut, skinned

3 eggs

a bunch of fresh parsley, chopped

¾ cup flour, plus extra to dust

2 cups bread crumbs

1¼ cups olive oil

sea salt and freshly ground black pepper

lemon wedges, to serve

hollandaise sauce, to serve

serves 4

Preheat the oven to 350°F and lightly oil a shallow ovenproof dish.

Cook the potatoes in boiling salted water for 20 minutes, Drain, return to the pan, and shake over low heat to dry off. Mash the potatoes, add the butter and milk, and mix well.

Put the fish into the prepared dish, cover with aluminum foil, and bake for 10 minutes. Let cool, then flake the fish into the potato. Beat one egg and add to the mixture, followed by the parsley and seasoning. Mix well.

Put the flour, bread crumbs, and remaining eggs in 3 separate bowls. Beat the eggs. Divide the fish mixture into 8 equal pieces and shape into patties. Dust each fish cake with flour, then use one hand to dip them into the egg; use the other hand to coat in the bread crumbs. Try to get an even coating.

Heat the oil and fry the fish cakes on each side for 5 minutes, or until golden. Serve with lemon wedges and hollandaise sauce.

The fish supper has been one of Britain's greatest exports. Crisp, flaky, freshly battered and fried fish (haddock in Scotland; cod in England) and plump, homemade french fries are cooked in beef dripping or good oil. They are then wrapped in newspaper and eaten in the street, on the quay, or carried home. This extremely simple batter is a favorite with many fish-and-chip shops. Typical accompaniments are brown sauce in Scotland, malt vinegar in England, plus salt, pickled onions, or gherkins.

fish supper

2 lb floury potatoes, cut lengthwise then crosswise into $\frac{1}{2}$-inch strips (keep in a bowl of ice water until ready to cook)

beef dripping or vegetable oil, for deep-frying

1$\frac{1}{2}$ lb haddock or cod fillets, skinned

sea salt and freshly ground black pepper

beer batter

1 cup all-purpose flour, sifted

1 teaspoon salt

1 cup flat beer or water

to serve (optional)

brown sauce or malt vinegar

pickled onions

gherkins

serves 4

To make the beer batter, put the flour, salt, and beer in a medium bowl and beat until smooth.

Drain the potato strips and pat dry with paper towels.

Put the beef dripping in a large, heavy-based, deep skillet to reach a depth of 1 inch and heat to 400°F—use a frying thermometer to check. Add half the potatoes to the skillet and fry, turning several times with a spatula, for 10–12 minutes. Remove, drain on sheets of crumpled paper towels, and keep hot in a moderate oven while you prepare the rest. Repeat with the remaining potatoes.

Divide the fish into 4 equal portions and pat dry on paper towels. Coat the pieces of fish in batter, turning them until well covered. Using tongs, add one portion at a time into the hot fat or oil. Cook until the batter is crisp and golden and the fish just opaque in the middle, about 3 minutes on each side (break one open with a fork to check). Drain on crumpled paper towels and keep hot. Repeat with the remaining pieces of fish.

Season and serve with your choice of accompaniments.

poultry and game

Cock-a-leekie is a Scottish classic, consisting mainly of chicken wings, giblets, and barley—an easy, economical "big soup" meal. In the past, in the small stone crofts (farm cottages), a whole chicken and its broth would bubble in a cauldron hung in the open fireplace. Prunes add extra sweetness, but brown sugar could do instead.

cock-a-leekie

1 lb large chicken wings

8 oz chicken giblets, excluding liver, or extra wings

8 oz stewing beef

1½ lb leeks, whites cut into ½-inch slices, green parts finely shredded

a small bunch of fresh thyme, tied with twine

a few fresh parsley stalks, plus 4 tablespoons chopped leaves, to serve

2 tablespoons pearl barley

2 onions, quartered

2 quarts boiling water

2 large potatoes, quartered

12 pitted prunes or 1 tablespoon brown sugar

sea salt and freshly ground black pepper

serves 4

Put the wings, giblets, beef, whites of the leeks, thyme, parsley stalks, pearl barley, and onions in a large saucepan and add the boiling water.

Bring to a boil, reduce the heat, cover, and simmer over medium heat for 50–60 minutes. For the last 15–20 minutes, add the potatoes, prunes, and finely shredded green parts of the leeks and cook until the potatoes are done.

Using tongs and a slotted spoon, carefully take the beef out of the saucepan and put it on a plate. Cut the beef into 4 pieces and return them to the soup. Taste and adjust the seasoning.

Ladle the soup into large bowls, sprinkle with the chopped parsley, and serve accompanied by crusty bread rolls.

variation If you prefer, you may omit the beef altogether, but adjust the seasonings carefully to balance the flavors.

1 medium free-range chicken

1 unwaxed lemon, thinly sliced

4 bay leaves

4 slices of bacon

sea salt and freshly ground black pepper

stuffing

2 garlic cloves, peeled and crushed

1 onion, finely diced

leaves from 4 sprigs of fresh thyme

1 large potato, coarsely grated

10 oz fresh sausage meat

peel and juice of 1 unwaxed lemon

gravy

2 tablespoons all-purpose flour

2 cups chicken stock

serves 4

For many people, the smell of roasting chicken conjures up childhood memories of a cozy Sunday at home. It's always worth cooking a larger bird than you need because the leftovers can be used in a pilaf or to make sandwiches. You can also use the carcass to make stock and freeze it. Three meals for the price of one bird!

roast chicken *with lemon, thyme, and potato stuffing*

Preheat the oven to 350°F. Lightly oil a roasting pan.

Take the chicken and carefully slide the lemon slices and bay leaves between the skin and the breast meat.

To make the stuffing, put the garlic, onion, thyme, potato, and sausage meat in a large bowl. Add the lemon peel and juice, season, and mix well. Cut any excess fat from the cavity of the chicken, then stuff.

Weigh your chicken to work out the cooking time: you should allow 20 minutes per pound, plus 20 minutes extra. Put the chicken in the prepared roasting pan and lay the slices of bacon over the breast. Put in the hot oven and cook for the time you have calculated. When the chicken is ready, remove it from the roasting pan and keep warm.

Now make the gravy. Add the flour to the pan and stir with a wooden spoon to combine with the fat and juices. Slowly pour in the chicken stock, stirring continuously to prevent lumps forming. Put the roasting pan directly on the heat and bring to a boil. When the mixture has thickened, remove it from the heat and season well. If you like a very smooth gravy, press it through a strainer with the back of a spoon.

Family tradition will dictate the best way to present a festive turkey. This recipe uses a fresh chestnut stuffing for the neck cavity. The appeal of roast turkey is as much in the many accompaniments as it is in the meat itself.

traditional roast turkey

1 turkey, 13–15 lb

1 stick salted butter

Chestnut Stuffing (page 106)

2 cups chicken or vegetable stock

sea salt and freshly ground
black pepper

to serve

Roast Potatoes (page 111)

Bread Sauce (page 106)

Cranberry Relish (page 107)

lightly boiled Brussels sprouts

broiled chipolatas

roasted bacon rolls

*squares of cheesecloth, paper, or
aluminum foil (enough to cover
the breast and drumsticks)*

serves 6

Preheat the oven to 425°F.

Wipe out the neck area and cavity of the turkey with a damp cloth and lightly season the inside. Spoon the Chestnut Stuffing into the neck cavity, allowing plenty of room for it to expand.

Put half the butter in a saucepan and melt gently. Spread the remaining butter all over the skin of the turkey. Soak the cheesecloth in the melted butter and drape over the bird, with a double layer of cheesecloth covering the drumsticks.

Put the bird in a large roasting pan in the middle of the oven. Roast for 40 minutes. Reduce the oven temperature to 335°F and baste now and every 30 minutes until cooked (remove and replace the cheesecloth as necessary). Roast at this temperature for just under 4 hours.

Raise the oven temperature to 425°F, remove the coverings, and roast for 30 minutes to crisp the skin. Remove the turkey from the oven, cover with a tent of aluminum foil, and let rest in a warm place while you cook the accompaniments.

Using oven gloves, tip out any free juices from the cavity, then lift the turkey onto a serving platter. Pour off the gravy juices from the pan, preferably into a gravy separator or pitcher to lift off the fat, then pour in the stock and heat. Serve with the turkey and all the accompaniments.

Ring the changes with this succulent roast goose, perfect as a Christmas lunch. The prunes and apples turn gorgeously soft and sticky after 4 hours inside the roasting bird. Serve with Roast Beets (page 117).

roast goose

1 goose, about 12 lb

2 cups pitted prunes

1 lb tart apples, peeled, cored, and quartered

⅓ cup red wine

1 tablespoon cornstarch, mixed with 1 tablespoon water

⅔–1¼ cups chicken stock

¼ cup cream

sea salt and freshly ground black pepper

an instant-read thermometer

serves 6

Dry the goose inside and out with paper towels, then rub with salt and pepper and prick the skin all over with a skewer or sharp-pronged fork.

Scald the prunes with boiling water and stuff the goose with the apples and prunes.

Put the goose breast-side up on a rack in a roasting pan. Put in a cold oven, turn to 325°F, and roast for 45 minutes. Add a little cold water to the pan and roast for 3½ hours or 20 minutes per pound. Take care not to let the water dry up—add extra as necessary. The goose is done when an instant-read thermometer reaches 180°F. Alternatively, the juices should run clear when you prick the leg at the thickest part. Waggle the leg bone a little—it should move in the socket. Transfer the bird to a platter.

Reserve 1 tablespoon of the goose fat, pour the gravy juices into a small bowl, and stir in the cornstarch mixture. Increase the oven temperature to 500°F. Return the goose to the roasting pan, pour 2 tablespoons cold water over the breast, and return the bird to the oven.

Pour the wine into a clean saucepan, add the reserved goose fat, bring to a boil, and reduce until syrupy. Add the gravy juices mixture and the stock and return to a boil, stirring all the time. Season well and stir in the cream.

1 venison saddle, about 4 lb,
boned and rolled

stock

½ onion, chopped

1 cup red wine

marinade

5 tablespoons softened butter or
¼ cup olive oil

12 juniper berries, crushed

½ teaspoon dried thyme

2 garlic cloves,
peeled and crushed

5 anchovies, well rinsed,
then chopped

1 tablespoon port

a strip of pork fat
or 3 slices of fatty bacon,
made into long rolls

3 sprigs of fresh rosemary

sea salt and freshly ground
black pepper

gravy

1 tablespoon cranberry jelly

1 tablespoon cornstarch, mixed
with ½ cup water

kitchen twine

an instant-read thermometer

serves 8–10

Venison is an umbrella word covering the meat of many kinds of deer. The saddle of these animals is almost always tender but it is still a good idea to tenderize the meat further by hanging it for a while. A good butcher will often do this for you.

marinated roast venison

Open the saddle and cut away all the loose trimmings around the rib area and any excess flank, leaving enough to wrap around the meat. To make a stock, put the trimmings, onion, red wine, and 2 cups water in a saucepan. Bring to a boil, reduce the heat, and simmer gently for 1 hour.

To make the marinade, put the butter, juniper berries, thyme, garlic, anchovies, and seasoning in a bowl and mix well. Put the opened saddle in a roasting pan, rub with half the marinade and sprinkle with the port. Arrange the rolled pork fat lengthwise along the backbone cavity, top with the sprigs of rosemary, close the meat up, and tie it with twine. Rub the outside with the rest of the marinade, wrap the meat in foil or parchment paper, and leave in a cool place for at least 3 hours.

Preheat the oven to 450°F.

Unwrap the meat and roast for 10 minutes, then reduce to 325°F for 45 minutes, or until an instant-read thermometer registers 150°F. Baste the meat with the pan juices 2–3 times during this period. Transfer the meat to a serving dish and keep it warm (discard the twine).

To make the gravy, put the roasting pan on top of the stove. Add the cranberry jelly and stock and let it boil until the jelly dissolves, then add the cornstarch mixture, return to a boil, season, and add any juices collected from the roast. Serve the gravy in a pitcher. Carve the meat straight across the grain, not lengthwise as is often done with a saddle.

Only very young rabbits should be roasted whole, giving the most tender pure white meat imaginable. Otherwise it is best to cut the meat into pieces, frying the legs in butter first to give them a bit of color, then roasting them with the saddle.

roast rabbit
with herbs and cider

4 wild rabbits, about 1 lb each
or 2 farmed ones

1 onion, chopped

1 carrot, sliced

1 bay leaf

12 slices of fatty bacon

1 stick butter

3 tip sprigs of fresh rosemary,
or 1 long one, broken into 3,
or 1 teaspoon dried rosemary

6–8 tip sprigs of fresh thyme,
2–3 whole sprigs,
or ½ teaspoon dried thyme

¾ cup hard cider

2 tablespoons heavy cream
(optional)

sea salt and freshly
ground black pepper

an instant-read thermometer

serves 4

First cut the legs and saddle off each rabbit and reserve with the kidneys. To make a stock, put the bones in a saucepan, add the onion, carrot, and bay leaf, cover with water, and simmer for about 1 hour. Strain off and reserve the stock, discard the bones, and reserve the onion and carrot.

Preheat the oven to 450°F.

Loosen the tough membrane around the saddles by sliding the point of a sharp knife along the backbone from under the neck end to the tail, freeing the meat underneath. Do one side at a time, then cut off and discard it. Cover the saddle with strips of bacon.

Melt the butter in a skillet, add the legs, and fry for about 5 minutes to give them a bit of color. Season with salt, pepper, rosemary, and thyme. Put the reserved onion and carrot in a roasting pan and set the legs and saddle on top. Roast for 15–20 minutes according to size or until an instant-read thermometer registers 160°F.

Add the kidneys to the pan used to brown the legs, adding a little extra butter if necessary. Fry gently until firm, then remove and set aside. Deglaze the pan with the cider, add the stock and the cream, if using, and reduce the gravy. Season to taste. Arrange the meat and kidneys on a serving dish and pour the sauce over the top.

Roast guinea fowl is a treat; half chicken, half game, it is full of flavor. Cutting poultry and meat into small pieces means that they roast very quickly and absorb other ingredients more directly, giving great finger-licking potential. This recipe makes for a quick, easy roast to serve for a special meal.

roast guinea fowl
with new potatoes and green beans

3 lb guinea fowl

2 tablespoons butter

1½ lb new potatoes

6 oz green beans

½ cup vegetable stock

sea salt

radicchio plumes, to serve (optional)

serves 4–6

If using a whole guinea fowl, cut in half lengthwise, then cut each half into 6 evenly sized pieces.

Arrange the guinea fowl in a large roasting pan, dot with butter, and sprinkle generously with salt. Cover with aluminum foil and let stand at room temperature for 1 hour.

Preheat the oven to 400°F.

Remove the foil and roast for 30 minutes, or until golden brown and tender, turning at least once.

Meanwhile, put the potatoes in a small saucepan of salted water and boil until tender, then drain. Cook the beans in the same way for about 8 minutes until al dente, then drain.

Add the potatoes and beans to the roasting dish and stir well to coat with the pan juices. Transfer the meat and vegetables to a serving plate.

Deglaze the pan with the stock, boil until reduced by half, then pour over the meat and vegetables. Serve with radicchio plumes, if using.

meat

Serve this with beef's stalwart companions—Yorkshire puddings, horseradish sauce, and lots of gravy.

roast beef
with all the trimmings

6½ lb bone-in beef rib roast (2–3 bones)

2 tablespoons all-purpose flour

1 tablespoon hot mustard powder

3 oz beef dripping, shortening, or ¼ cup olive oil

3 onions, quartered

8–10 potatoes, cut into chunks and parboiled

5–6 parsnips, halved lengthwise

sea salt and freshly ground black pepper

to serve

Yorkshire Puddings (page 125)

Horseradish Sauce (page 125)

3 lb green vegetable, such as cabbage, sliced and steamed or boiled

1 recipe Gravy (page 107)

an instant-read thermometer

serves 8–10

Preheat the oven to 475°F.

Season the meat, mix the flour and the mustard, and pat it onto the beef fat. Put the dripping in a roasting pan, put the onions in the middle and set the beef, fat-side up, on top. Put the potatoes and parsnips around the meat and put the pan in the oven. Roast for 35 minutes.

Reduce the oven temperature to 375°F, baste the beef, and turn the potatoes and parsnips in the fat. Keep basting and turning the vegetables every 15 minutes. Roast for 70 minutes.

Increase the oven temperature to 475°F and roast for a further 10 minutes.

Remove the beef from the oven, or when an instant-read thermometer registers 175°F (or a little below if you like beef very rare). Lift the beef onto a serving dish and set aside in a warm place for 20 minutes. It will go on cooking as it rests.

Spoon off the fat from the roasting pan and retain it for another time, or use for the Yorkshire puddings.

Serve the beef with the horseradish sauce, Yorkshire puddings, green vegetables and gravy.

This dish is absolutely delicious, a real winner for either an informal dinner party or just a midweek meal. What's more, it's an absolute breeze to make. Stilton is the ideal accompaniment to the succulent steak.

stilton steaks *with sweet potato and garlic mash*

1¼ lb sweet potatoes, peeled and cut into chunks

3½ oz potatoes, peeled and cut into chunks

2–3 garlic cloves, peeled

4 sirloin steaks, about 8 oz each

2½ oz Stilton cheese

1 tablespoon olive oil

6 fresh oregano sprigs, chopped

sea salt and freshly ground black pepper

serves 4

Bring a large saucepan of lightly salted water to a boil. Add the sweet potatoes, potatoes, and garlic. Cook until tender, about 20 minutes.

Cook the steaks under a hot broiler for 8–10 minutes, depending on personal preference, turning once halfway through the cooking time. Divide the Stilton into 4 equal pieces and crumble over the top of the steaks a couple of minutes before removing them from the broiler. Keep them warm in a low oven.

Drain the potatoes, reserving ¼ cup of the cooking water. Return the potatoes and garlic to the warm saucepan. Add the oil and most of the oregano and season with salt and pepper. Mash well, adding a little of the reserved cooking water to moisten, if necessary.

Divide the mash between 4 warm serving plates and put the Stilton steaks on top. Sprinkle with some oregano leaves and serve immediately.

variation When in season, replace the potatoes with the equivalent weight of peeled Jerusalem artichokes.

Think of chilly, dark evenings and this is exactly what you'd want to eat. The featherlight dumplings nestling in the rich, savory casserole will have everyone demanding more. A staple of British cooking.

beef and carrot casserole
with cheesy dumplings

1 tablespoon olive oil

2 garlic cloves, peeled and crushed

1 onion, diced

2 celery stalks, diced

2 lb chuck steak, cut into cubes

1²⁄₃ cups beef stock

¾ cup red wine

2 bay leaves

4 carrots, cut into small chunks

2 tablespoons all-purpose flour

sea salt and freshly ground black pepper

dumplings

1½ cups all-purpose flour

⅓ cup shortening

1 teaspoon baking powder

½ cup grated sharp Cheddar cheese

serves 4–6

Heat the olive oil in a large casserole dish, add the garlic, onion, and celery, and sauté for 4 minutes. Transfer to a plate. Put the beef in the casserole, increase the heat, and sauté for 5 minutes, stirring frequently. When the beef is cooked, return the onion mixture to the casserole. Add the stock, red wine, seasoning, and bay leaves, bring to a boil, then reduce the heat to a gentle simmer. Cover and cook for 1½ hours.

To make the dumplings, place the flour and baking powder in a bowl and rub in the shortening until it resembles bread crumbs. Add the cheese, mixing it in with a knife. Add ¼–⅓ cup water and use your hands to bring the mixture together and form a dough. Divide into 8 equal pieces and roll into balls.

Remove the casserole from the heat for 5 minutes, then sift in the flour and stir to thicken the gravy. Return to the heat, add the carrots, and stir until the casserole comes to a simmer. Place the dumplings on top, cover, and cook for a further 20 minutes.

Here's an Irish twist on a Belgian classic. Carbonnade is usually flavored with beer but a good Irish stout works particularly well, adding an extra dimension of bitterness to counter the naturally sweet gravy. Lots of shallots also add to the sweetness here. Serve with mounds of creamy mashed potatoes.

irish carbonnade

2 tablespoons duck or goose fat, or peanut, canola, or safflower oil

1½ lb flank steak, cut into 1-inch cubes

3 tablespoons sugar

1 onion, chopped

2 tablespoons all-purpose flour

12 shallots

2 cups hot beef stock

1½ cups stout, such as Guinness

2 tablespoons red wine vinegar

3 cloves

2 bay leaves

sea salt and freshly ground black pepper

serves 4

Heat the fat in a large skillet. Season the meat, add to the skillet, and sauté until brown all over. Transfer to a large, flameproof casserole dish.

Add the sugar to the skillet and let it cook until it becomes a good chestnut color. Add the onion, flour, and shallots and mix well for about 30 seconds. Stir in the stock and stout. Bring to a boil and cook for 1 minute. Add the vinegar, cloves, bay leaves, and a little more seasoning, then pour it all over the meat in the casserole dish. Mix well.

Cover the casserole and leave to simmer very gently on the stove or in a preheated oven at 325°F for 1½–2 hours. Remove from the heat or the oven and pour off the liquid into a separate saucepan or skillet. Bring to the boil and simmer to reduce the liquid to a coating consistency. Return it to the casserole and serve.

A British classic, with many subtle variations. This one is served with a rich mustard sauce to complete the dish.

beef wellington

¼ cup olive oil

3 shallots, finely chopped

2 garlic cloves,
peeled and chopped

6 oz portobello mushrooms, sliced

3½ lb beef tenderloin, trimmed

1 lb puff or shortcrust
pastry dough

2 eggs, beaten

sea salt and freshly ground
black pepper

mustard sauce

2 tablespoons mustard

2 tablespoons grainy mustard

½ cup white wine

1¾ cups heavy cream

serves 8

Put 2 tablespoons of the olive oil into a skillet, heat gently, then add the shallots, garlic, and mushrooms. Cook for 15 minutes, stirring frequently, until soft but not brown and all the liquid has evaporated. Season, let cool, then chill.

Preheat the oven to 425°F.

Put 1 tablespoon of the remaining oil in a roasting pan and heat in the oven for 5 minutes. Rub the beef with the remaining oil and some seasoning, and transfer to the roasting pan. Cook for 15 minutes, then transfer to a plate, reserving the meat juices, and let cool.

Roll out the dough to a rectangle large enough to wrap around the fillet. Brush lightly with the beaten eggs. Spoon the mushroom mixture evenly over the dough, leaving a 2-inch border all around. Put the cold beef fillet in the middle of the dough, on top of the mushrooms, and roll the dough around the fillet. Try not to have too much dough at the ends, and trim to avoid areas of double dough. Turn the package so that the seam is underneath, and transfer to a lightly oiled baking sheet. Brush all over with the beaten eggs and chill for 2 hours.

Preheat the oven to 400°F.

Roast for 20 minutes. Reduce the heat to 350°F and cook for 15 minutes for rare, 35 minutes for medium, and 50 minutes for well done. If you are cooking to well done, you may need to reduce the oven temperature to prevent the dough from burning.

Put the mustards, wine, heavy cream, and reserved roasting juices into a pan. Bring to a boil, then simmer for 5 minutes. Serve with the beef.

Steak and kidney pudding is British food at its best. Serve wrapped in a linen napkin, with a pitcher of extra stock.

steak and kidney pudding

1 lb beef kidney, trimmed of any membrane, then cut into 1-inch chunks

¼ cup all-purpose flour

1 teaspoon sea salt

1 teaspoon freshly ground black pepper

1½ lb boneless shank crosscuts or chuck steak, cut into 1-inch cubes

2 onions, chopped

2¾ cups beef stock or water

suet crust

3½ cups self-rising flour

1 teaspoon sea salt

2¼ cups suet or shortening

a heatproof ceramic bowl, 9-cup capacity

kitchen twine

serves 4–6

To make the suet crust, put the flour, salt, and suet in a bowl and add about 2¾ cups water, or enough to make a firm mixture. Mix to form a ball. Roll two-thirds of the dough out to a disk 16 inches in diameter. Cut out a wedge from the disk. Line the bowl, letting the dough overlap the edges by 1 inch (trim back any excess). Seal any joins with water.

Put the flour, salt, and pepper into a plastic bag, seal, and shake. Add the steak and kidney to the bag and shake it vigorously until all the meat is evenly coated with the seasoned flour. Remove the meat from the bag, shake off any excess flour, and transfer to the bowl. Sprinkle with onion.

Heat the stock, season to taste, then pour about half of it over the meat to cover it. Reserve the remaining stock. Roll out the remaining dough to make a disk just big enough to cover the top of the bowl.

Fold the overlapping edges of the dough inward over the top of the meat and brush the top edge with water. Put the dough lid on top and crimp the edges inside the rim to seal the pudding.

Fold a large sheet of aluminum foil to make a pleat down the middle. Put on top of the bowl and tie a length of twine firmly around the edge, under the lip of the bowl. Tie a "handle" of twine from side to side to make the pudding easier to lift in and out of the pan.

Lower into a casserole dish, three-quarters fill the pan with boiling water, and cover with a lid. Return to a boil, reduce the heat, and simmer for 4 hours (for chuck meat) or 6 hours (for shank meat), topping it up with boiling water from time to time. After the first helping has been served, gently mix in the rest of the stock to thin the gravy for second helpings.

2 oz dried wild mushrooms

⅓ cup olive oil or dripping

1 onion, finely chopped

3 garlic cloves,
peeled and chopped

1 large carrot, finely chopped

2 celery stalks, finely chopped

4 oz cubed fatty bacon

8 juniper berries, crushed

3 bay leaves

2 tablespoons chopped
fresh thyme

2 tablespoons all-purpose flour

2 lb stewing beef, trimmed
and cut into large cubes

1¼ cups red wine

2 tablespoons cranberry or
red currant jelly

1¼ lb puff pastry sheets

1 egg, beaten

sea salt and freshly ground
black pepper

*6 individual pie dishes or
1 large pie dish*

2 baking sheets

serves 6

This glorious recipe can be made as a large pie, or as individual pies for a special occasion. It can be made ahead of time—even frozen. Make the stew in advance, top with dough, and refrigerate until ready to cook.

beef and mushroom pies

Put the mushrooms in a bowl, just cover with hot water, and let soak for 30 minutes. Meanwhile, heat half the olive oil in a large casserole dish, add the onion, garlic, carrot, and celery, and cook for 5–10 minutes until softening. Stir in the bacon and fry with the vegetables until just beginning to brown. Add the juniper berries, bay leaves, and thyme, sprinkle in the flour, mix well, and set aside.

Heat the remaining olive oil in a large skillet and fry the beef quickly (in batches) on all sides until crusty and brown. Transfer to the casserole as you go. When done, deglaze the skillet with the wine, let bubble, then scrape up the sediment from the bottom of the skillet. Pour over the meat and vegetables.

Drain the mushrooms and add to the casserole with ⅔ cup of the soaking water and the cranberry jelly. Season, then stir. Bring to a boil on top of the stove, then simmer for 1½ hours. Let cool overnight.

Next day, preheat the oven to 425°F.

Spoon the stew into 6 individual pie dishes. Cut out 6 circles of dough, a good 1 inch wider than the dishes. Brush the edges of the dishes with beaten egg. Sit the dough on top of the rim and press over the edge to seal tightly. Brush with more beaten egg, but don't pierce the tops (the steam must be trapped inside). Set the pies on 2 baking sheets and chill for 30 minutes or until ready to bake. Bake for 20–25 minutes, or until the dough is risen, crisp, and golden brown. Serve hot.

8 oz pork loin, diced

4 oz pork belly, diced

3 slices of bacon, diced

1 oz chicken livers

1 small onion, minced

1 tablespoon chopped
fresh sage leaves

1 small garlic clove, peeled
and crushed

a pinch of ground mace
or nutmeg

1 red apple, peeled, cored,
and diced

sea salt and freshly ground
black pepper

pie crust

2½ cups all-purpose flour,
plus extra to dust

1½ teaspoons salt

¼ cup vegetable shortening

glaze

1 egg yolk mixed with
1 tablespoon milk

1 jam jar

kitchen twine

*6 pieces of wax paper,
about 12 x 3 inches each*

serves 6

Pork and apple is a delicious combination. These pies are easily transportable and make a wonderful picnic dish.

mini pork and apple pies

Preheat the oven to 375°F.

Put the pork loin, pork belly, bacon, and chicken livers in a food processor and blend briefly to grind the meat. Transfer to a bowl and mix in the onion, sage, garlic, mace, and a little seasoning. Set aside.

To make the pie crust, sift the flour and salt in a bowl. Put the shortening and ½ cup water in a saucepan and heat gently until the fat melts and the water comes to a boil. Pour the liquid into the flour and, using a wooden spoon, gently draw the flour into the liquid to form a soft dough. Let cool for a few minutes and, as soon as the dough is cool enough to handle, knead lightly in the bowl until smooth.

Divide the dough into 8 pieces and roll 6 of these into 5-inch disks. Invert them, one at a time over an upturned jam jar. Wrap a piece of wax paper around the outside, then tie around the middle with twine.

Turn the whole thing over so the dough is sitting flat. Carefully work the jar up and out of the pie crust (you may need to slip a small palette knife down between the dough and the jar to loosen it).

Divide the pork filling into 6 portions and put 1 portion in each pie. Put the diced apple on top. Roll out the remaining 2 pieces of dough and, using a cookie cutter, cut 3 disks from each piece the same size as the top of the pies. Put a pastry disk on top of each pie, press the edges to seal, then turn the edges inward and over to form a rim.

Brush the tops of the pies with egg-milk glaze. Pierce each one with a fork to let the steam escape. Transfer to a large baking sheet and bake for 45–50 minutes, or until golden. Remove from the oven, transfer to a wire rack, let cool, and serve cold.

The original humble British comfort food, toad-in-the-hole makes a great Friday night dinner dish.

sausage and bacon toad-in-the-hole

1½ cups all-purpose flour

2 eggs

⅔ cup milk

8 slices of bacon

2 lb sausages

2 red onions, cut into wedges

sea salt and freshly ground black pepper

serves 4–6

Put the flour in a mixing bowl and make a well in the center. Beat the eggs, milk, and ⅔ cup water together and pour into the well. Stir carefully with a wooden spoon until you have a smooth batter. Let rest for 30 minutes.

Preheat the oven to 425°F. Grease a large roasting pan or 4–6 individual dishes and place in the oven.

Wrap the bacon around the sausages and place in the hot roasting pan or dishes. Add the onion, then pour in the batter. Return to the oven and bake for 30 minutes without opening the door. The batter should be light and well risen.

Apple and blackberry is a classic fall combination best known as a crumble or pie filling but it also works surprisingly well with pork. Be careful not to burn the pan juices, which you then pour over the finished dish.

pork steaks *with apple and blackberry compote*

4 large pork steaks, about 8 oz each

4 tablespoons butter

12 large fresh sage leaves

sea salt and freshly ground black pepper

apple and blackberry compote

8 oz cooking apples, cored and cut into thin wedges

⅔ cup blackberries

2 tablespoons sugar

freshly squeezed juice of ½ lemon

3 juniper berries

serves 4

To make the apple and blackberry compote, put the apples, blackberries, sugar, lemon juice, juniper berries, and 2 tablespoons water into a saucepan. Cover and cook gently until the fruits have softened. Remove the lid and simmer until the juices have evaporated. Remove from the heat, but keep the mixture warm.

Season the pork steaks. Melt the butter in a large skillet and, as soon as it stops foaming, add the pork. Cook over medium heat for 3–4 minutes on each side until brown and cooked through.

Let rest in a warm oven for 5 minutes. Meanwhile add the sage to the same skillet and fry for a few seconds until crispy. Serve the steaks topped with a spoonful of the compote, the sage leaves, and pan juices.

Sometimes this cut is sold without the skin, so it is a good idea to wrap strips of bacon around the meat. The idea is to release some gelatin into the wine to emulsify and combine all the ingredients when you make the gravy. Half a teaspoon of dissolved gelatin added at the end has the same effect, though not the same flavor.

loin of pork *with a herb crust*

Make several small incisions on the underside of the meat and insert the slivers of garlic (use more if you like). Season the meat. Lay the slices of bacon in a roasting pan.

Pour the wine into a plastic bag, add 1 tablespoon of the olive oil, half the thyme, some salt, then finally add the meat. Close the bag, excluding as much air as possible and refrigerate in a dish for at least 2 hours.

Preheat the oven to 500°F.

Put the meat on top of the bacon in the roasting pan and put in the oven, then reduce the temperature to 350°F. Baste with the marinade.

Heat the remaining oil in a pan and add the crushed garlic. When it begins to color, add the bread crumbs, parsley, and remaining thyme.

After 1 hour, remove the meat from the oven and pack the seasoned crumbs on top. Baste carefully with the pan juices. Return to the oven and cook for a further 40 minutes or until an instant-read thermometer registers 175°F. Lift the meat onto a platter and pour the stock into the pan. Bring to a boil on top of the stove. Season to taste and melt in the jelly. Serve separately in a pitcher.

3 lb loin of pork, chined and trimmed

2 garlic cloves, 1 cut into slivers, 1 crushed

6–7 slices of fatty bacon (optional)

⅔ cup red wine

2 tablespoons olive or safflower oil

2 teaspoons chopped fresh thyme

1⅓ cups fresh bread crumbs

1 tablespoon chopped fresh flatleaf parsley

1 cup beef stock

2 teaspoons cranberry jelly

sea salt and freshly ground black pepper

an instant-read thermometer

serves 4

4 lb pork arm roast or Boston butt, with rind if possible, and scored

1 teaspoon sea salt

2 tablespoons olive oil, to glaze

stuffing

1 onion, finely chopped

1 green apple, such as Granny Smith, cut into small pieces

2 celery stalks, finely chopped

½ cup cashews, chopped

4 tablespoons unsalted butter

2 teaspoons chopped fresh sage leaves

grated peel and freshly squeezed juice of 1 unwaxed lemon

5 cups fresh bread crumbs

cider gravy

½ cup cider vinegar

1 cup water or chicken stock

a roasting pan with a rack

a baking sheet with sides

an instant-read thermometer (optional)

serves 6

This is an ideal cut of pork to serve with crackling. If you can't get the meat with its outer skin on, simply bone and stuff it, and miss out the high roasting part at the end.

rolled pork roast
with sage and onion stuffing

To make the stuffing, put the onion, apple, celery, cashews, butter, sage, lemon peel and juice, and bread crumbs in a bowl. Mix well.

Season the inside of the pork with the salt, then spread the stuffing over that side, roll up the meat, and tie it with twine to make a good shape. Brush with the oil and put it on a rack in a roasting pan. Add 1 cup water. Put it in a cold oven, turn the heat to 425°F and roast for 30 minutes.

Reduce the oven temperature to 325°F. Cook for another 1½ hours or until an instant-read thermometer registers 175°F. Transfer the meat to a baking sheet with sides. Do not baste during this time (unless the meat is rindless, in which case, baste 3–4 times during cooking). Raise the oven temperature to maximum and return the meat to the very hot oven for 20 minutes to crisp the surface.

Meanwhile, make the gravy by deglazing the roasting pan with the vinegar and reducing it well. Add the water or stock, bring to a boil, then season with salt if necessary. Serve in a sauceboat. When the meat is ready, transfer it to a carving platter and let rest for 10–20 minutes before carving in fairly thick slices.

This lamb is cooked on a bed of rosemary and onions until it is completely tender all the way through—and the onions are melting into the rosemary gravy. Purée the meat juices with the soft onions for a creamy sauce.

pot roast leg of lamb
with rosemary and onion gravy

3 lb leg of lamb

2 tablespoons olive oil

3 garlic cloves, peeled and crushed

2 tablespoons chopped fresh rosemary

3 large fresh rosemary sprigs

2 bay leaves

4 large onions, thinly sliced

1¼ cups dry white wine

2 teaspoons mustard

sea salt and freshly ground black pepper

mint sauce

a large bunch of fresh mint, finely chopped

1 teaspoon caster sugar

2 tablespoons white wine vinegar

serves 6

Trim the lamb of any excess fat. Heat the olive oil in a casserole dish in which the lamb will fit snugly. Add the lamb and brown it all over. Transfer to a plate and let cool.

Preheat the oven to 325°F. Meanwhile, to make the mint sauce, put the ingredients in a bowl and let steep for at least 1 hour.

Crush the garlic and chopped rosemary together with a mortar and pestle. Using a small sharp knife, make little incisions all over the lamb. Push the paste well into these incisions. Season well.

Put the rosemary sprigs, bay leaves, and onions in the casserole and put the lamb on top. Mix the wine with the mustard, then pour into the casserole. Bring to a boil, cover tightly, then cook in the oven for 1½ hours, turning the lamb over twice.

Raise the oven temperature to 400°F and remove the lid from the casserole dish. Cook for another 30 minutes.

Carefully remove the lamb to a serving dish and keep it warm. Skim the fat from the cooking juices and remove the bay leaves and rosemary sprigs. Add a little water if too thick, then bring to a boil, scraping the bottom of the pan to mix in the sediment. Pour the sauce into a blender or food processor and blend until smooth. Season to taste. Serve with the freshly made mint sauce.

The preparation and cooking of this dish can be spread over three days, which makes it perfect for Sunday lunch.

lamb shanks *with red wine, rosemary, and garlic*

6 even-sized lamb shanks, about 4½ lb in total

1 large onion, thinly sliced

3 carrots, cut into thin sticks

4 garlic cloves, peeled and thinly sliced

2–3 sprigs of fresh rosemary

½ teaspoon black peppercorns

1 bottle robust red wine, 750 ml, such as Shiraz, Malbec, or Zinfandel, plus ½ cup to finish

¼ cup olive oil

2 cups strained tomatoes

sea salt and freshly ground black pepper

Mashed Potatoes (page 112), to serve

a large, heavyweight plastic bag

serves 6

Put the lamb in a large, heavyweight plastic bag. Add the onion, carrots, garlic, rosemary, and peppercorns. Pour in the wine, secure the bag, put in a bowl, and refrigerate overnight.

The next day, remove the lamb from the marinade, pat dry with paper towels, and season. Strain the marinade into a large bowl and reserve the vegetables. Preheat the oven to 325°F.

Heat half the olive oil in a large casserole dish, add the lamb, and brown evenly, in batches. Remove the lamb and set it aside. Add the remaining oil to the casserole, then add the reserved vegetables and fry briefly until they begin to soften. Add a few tablespoons of the marinade and let it bubble up, incorporating any caramelized juices that have stuck to the casserole. Stir in the strained tomatoes and the rest of the marinade, then return the lamb to the pan. Spoon over the vegetables and sauce and bring to simmering point. Cover the meat tightly with parchment paper, cover with the lid, and cook in the oven for 1¾–2 hours. Remove the lid and paper and cook for a further 30 minutes. Remove the rosemary sprigs, let cool, cover, and refrigerate overnight.

The next day, remove any fat that has accumulated on the surface. Reheat gently on the stove until the sauce comes to simmering point. If the sauce isn't thick enough, remove the lamb from the pan, simmer the sauce until it thickens, then return the lamb to the pan. Add the remaining ½ cup wine and simmer for a further 15 minutes. Season to taste. Serve with mashed potatoes.

Inspired by thrift, this dish has transcended its humble origins and become a firm favorite around the world. The golden potato topping hides tender lamb in heavenly gravy. A real winter warmer.

lancashire hotpot

2 tablespoons olive oil

2 lb stewing lamb, cut into 2-inch pieces

1 onion, diced

2 carrots, diced

4 celery stalks, diced

2 leeks, thinly sliced

2 tablespoons all-purpose flour

1 tablespoon Worcestershire sauce

2 lb potatoes, unpeeled

sea salt and freshly ground black pepper

serves 4–6

Heat the olive oil in a large, flameproof casserole dish, add the lamb, and brown all over. Transfer to a plate. Reduce the heat under the casserole, add all the vegetables, then sauté for 10 minutes, stirring frequently.

Remove the casserole from the heat, add the meat, then sprinkle in the flour and mix well. Pour in just enough hot water to cover the meat and vegetables, stir well, and return to the heat.

Preheat the oven to 350°F.

Bring the casserole to a boil, stirring frequently as the gravy thickens. Season and add the Worcestershire sauce. Remove from the heat.

Slice the potatoes thinly by hand or with a mandolin. Layer them carefully over the meat and vegetables, covering them completely. Place in the oven and cook for 2 hours. The potatoes should be golden on top and the gravy bubbling up around the sides.

2 tablespoons unsalted butter or
2 tablespoons safflower oil

2 onions, chopped

2 garlic cloves

1½ lb ground beef

3 slices of bacon, finely chopped

½ cup dry white wine

a handful of fresh flatleaf
parsley, chopped

a fresh thyme sprig,
leaves stripped

2 tablespoons tomato paste

2 oz freshly grated
Cheddar cheese

sea salt and freshly ground
black pepper

mashed potato

4 lb potatoes

1 bay leaf

1 cup hot milk

1 stick unsalted butter, cubed

sea salt

a baking dish,
about 12 inches long

serves 4–6

The traditional recipe calls for leftover cooked beef, so use that if you have some, but ground beef that has been well seasoned and cooked in a bit of wine comes a close second. Serve with a fruity red wine.

cottage pie

Preheat the oven to 400°F.

To make the mashed potato, put the potatoes and bay leaf in a saucepan of cold water. Bring to a boil, add salt, and cook until tender. Drain.

Put the potatoes in a large bowl and mash coarsely with a wooden spoon. Using an electric mixer, gradually add the milk and butter, beating until the mixture is smooth. Add salt and beat well. If the potatoes are very dry, add more milk. Taste, then add more butter and/or salt as necessary and set aside.

Heat the butter in a skillet, add the onions, and cook over high heat until just brown, 3–5 minutes. Add the garlic, beef, and bacon and cook until almost completely brown. Add the wine and cook until almost evaporated. Stir in the parsley, thyme leaves, and tomato paste. Season to taste.

Spread the beef mixture over the prepared baking dish and level with a spoon. Spread with the potatoes. Sprinkle with the cheese and bake in the oven until golden, about 25–30 minutes.

bread sauce

½ onion, finely chopped

½ teaspoon dried thyme

3 whole cloves

2 cups milk

2 cups fresh white bread crumbs

5 tablespoons unsalted butter

2 tablespoons heavy cream

sea salt and freshly ground
black pepper

serves 8–10

Put the onion, thyme, cloves, and
milk in a saucepan. Bring gently
to a boil. Simmer for 5 minutes.
Remove from the heat and leave
for 1 hour. Remove the cloves.
Add the bread crumbs, butter, and
cream. Reheat until nearly boiling.
Stir well, then season to taste. Set
aside for 10 minutes to thicken.

chestnut stuffing

for turkey or goose

14 oz fresh chestnuts (7 oz peeled
and cooked) or 7 oz vacuum-packed
chestnuts, ready peeled and cooked

1 cup milk (if using fresh chestnuts)

4 oz sausages or sausage meat

2 tablespoons olive oil

1 onion, chopped

6 oz turkey liver, chopped
(if unavailable, use chicken livers)

2 oz bacon, finely chopped

1 tablespoon chopped fresh flatleaf
parsley or marjoram (optional)

sea salt and freshly ground
black pepper

makes about 3 cups stuffing

If the chestnuts are fresh, they
must first be boiled to soften the
shell, then peeled while still hot
(wear rubber gloves to protect
your fingers).

Put the peeled fresh chestnuts in
a saucepan, cover with the milk,
and simmer gently until softened,
probably 30 minutes, but it can
take up to 1 hour if they are old.
Strain them if necessary, weigh out
7 oz, and put in a bowl.

Crumble the cooked chestnuts
with your fingers and use the
sausage meat to bind them.

Heat the oil in a skillet, add the
onion, liver, and bacon, and fry
gently until the liver is firm. Stir
in the parsley and cook until the
mixture begins to brown. Add to
the chestnuts and season to taste.

note This stuffing may also be
cooked separately from the bird.
Form into balls and cook in a
baking dish at 400°F for about
20 minutes.

wine gravy

2 tablespoons fat from the roasting
pan used to roast the meat

¼ cup red wine

1 tablespoon all-purpose flour (or
more if you like a thicker gravy)

2 cups well-flavored stock or water

sea salt and freshly ground
black pepper

serves 4–6

Put the roasting pan on top of the
stove, heat the fat, add the wine,
and reduce to 3 tablespoons. Add
the flour, stir well, then pour in
the stock. Stir constantly over low
heat until the mixture boils.
Season. Strain into a clean pan
and reheat if necessary.

cranberry relish

1 cup fresh cranberries

½ cup cider vinegar

about 1 inch fresh ginger, grated

½ cinnamon stick

2 juniper berries, crushed

2 cloves

¼ cup moist brown sugar

makes about 1 cup relish

Put all the ingredients, except the
sugar, in a pan and simmer until
the berries collapse (add water if
it looks like drying out). Add the
sugar and cook for 20 minutes.
Remove the cloves and cinnamon
stick. It should be like a loose jam.
If not, simmer a little longer.

gravy

1 tablespoon fat from the roasting
pan used to roast the meat

1 onion, thinly sliced

1 cup good beef stock, or stock
to suit the roast meat or poultry

2 teaspoons cornstarch, mixed with
2 teaspoons cold water

sea salt and freshly ground
black pepper

serves 4–6

Put the roasting pan on top of the
stove, heat the fat, add the onion.
and cook slowly over low heat
until brown, about 30 minutes.
Add the stock and cornstarch
mixture, then season to taste.
Bring to a boil and simmer for
a couple of minutes.

on the side

Every good roast needs the traditional accompaniments to take it to the next level of deliciousness. Roast potatoes are always a favorite at the Sunday lunch table.

roast potatoes

12–16 potatoes, peeled

4 tablespoons duck or goose fat, or olive oil

serves 4

Preheat the oven to 350°F.

Parboil the potatoes in salted boiling water for 12 minutes, then drain and shake in the colander to roughen up the outsides.

Heat the fat in a large roasting pan in the oven and, when very hot, carefully add the potatoes, turning to coat them in the hot oil. Return to the oven and cook for 40 minutes. Do not disturb them before that or you will spoil their chances of crisping up. Turn them and cook for another 20 minutes.

Mashed potatoes scented with mellowed garlic, cream cheese, and good olive oil, are blissful. They marry well with fish but they seem to flatter most meat, poultry, and game dishes as well. Use large, floury-textured potatoes for mash—or even waxy if you prefer.

mashed potatoes

2¾ lb potatoes, such as Yukon Gold

2 whole heads of garlic, pierced all over with a fork

¼ cup cream cheese

¼ cup extra virgin olive oil

sea salt and freshly ground black pepper

serves 4–6

If large, cut the peeled potatoes into halves or quarters lengthwise. Otherwise, leave whole. Put them in a medium saucepan with the whole heads of garlic and 2 teaspoons sea salt, cover with boiling water, return to a boil, and cook for 18–25 minutes, or until tender.

Drain the saucepan well and return the potatoes to the still-hot, dry pan. Slice off the top of the garlic heads, squeeze out the soft purée, and add it to the potatoes. Add the cream cheese and extra virgin olive oil. Mash well with a potato masher or large fork or press through a potato ricer. Beat with a wooden spoon until creamy, then season to taste.

Pure comfort food, champ and colcannon are an inextricable part of Irish childhood memories. Dip each forkful of potato in the little pool of butter before eating.

champ

Put the potatoes in boiling salted water and cook for 20–25 minutes, or until tender. Drain well.

Put the scallions in a saucepan with the milk, bring to a boil, then simmer for 2–3 minutes. Remove from the heat and let infuse for 10 minutes.

Mash the potatoes using a potato ricer, beat in the milk and scallion mixture, then the butter and some seasoning. Put in a clean pan and reheat. To serve, spoon into small bowls in mounds, make a hollow in the top, and insert more butter and blue cheese (if using).

1½ lb floury potatoes, peeled and cut into large chunks

10 scallions, including the green tops, chopped

1¼ cups milk

3½ tablespoons butter, plus extra to serve

7 oz blue cheese, crumbled (optional)

salt and freshly ground black pepper

serves 4

variations **Colcannon, Ireland:** Kale, cabbage, or other leafy green vegetable is used instead of the scallion and cheese. It is served in the same way as champ, or formed into little cakes and fried in butter to form a crunchy crust.

Clapshot, Scotland: Follow the recipe for champ. Omit the cheese and add 1½ lb boiled, mashed rutabagas. Chives or bacon fat may also be added. The chopped scallions are optional.

Rumbledethumps, Scottish Borders: 1½ lb each of cooked potatoes and cabbage are thumped (mashed) then rumbled (mixed) with ground pepper and 1 stick butter, topped with cheese, and grilled until brown.

Punchnep, Wales: Half-and-half mashed turnips (neps) and potatoes are heaped into a mound and studded with hollows, which are then filled with cream.

This side dish is as good hot as it is at room temperature. When served hot, it also goes well with roast meat, especially lamb. Cooled, serve as part of a salad selection or a light meal, with a chunk of feta cheese, either crumbled over, or served whole to slice as needed.

roast beets

6 beets, about 1½ lb

3 tablespoons balsamic vinegar

2 tablespoons extra virgin olive oil

a small handful of fresh flatleaf parsley, chopped

a small handful of fresh oregano or dill, chopped

a fresh mint sprig, leaves chopped

coarse sea salt

serves 2–4

Preheat the oven to 400°F.

Peel the beets and trim the stems to about 1 inch (don't worry about your fingers, the pink soon goes away). Cut into 4–6 wedges, depending on size. Put the wedges in a baking dish that will hold them in a single layer. Add the vinegar, oil, parsley, oregano, mint, and a good pinch of salt. Toss well.

Cover the dish with aluminum foil and roast for 30 minutes. Remove the foil and continue roasting until just tender when pierced with a knife, about 20 minutes more. There should still be some liquid in the dish; if this evaporates too quickly, add a spoonful or so of water during cooking. Serve hot or at room temperature.

Be sure to use a sweet eating apple for this recipe. The cooking variety turns to a purée and spoils the roasting effect. Celery root must be thickly peeled to remove the tough outer skin. Choose young celery root, because older ones develop a soft, spongy center, unlike parsnips, which develop woody cores. Ideally, the centers of both vegetables should be cut away before cooking.

roast apples and celery root or parsnips

2 tablespoons olive oil

½ teaspoon dried sage

½ teaspoon salt

1 eating apple, cut into wedges

1 celery root or 2 parsnips, about 12 oz, peeled and cut into wedges

1 tablespoon chopped fresh flatleaf parsley

serves 4

Preheat the oven to 425°F.

Put the oil, sage, and salt in a plastic bag, then add the apple and celery root or parsnips. Roll them around until well coated with oil. Empty the bag onto a baking sheet and roast for 30 minutes, turning the vegetables every 10 minutes. Sprinkle with parsley, mix well, and serve.

variation **Parsnip chips:** Slice 1 lb parsnips into thin rounds and coat with olive oil and seasoning. Spread them out on a baking sheet and roast until brown and crisp. Serve with any roast, especially game.

This recipe is a very elegant way to dress up a rustic vegetable. It seems to go best with poultry and potatoes, both roasted. In fact, it's an idea to make extra cabbage and potatoes because they can be mashed together the next day, formed into patties, and fried in a mix of butter and olive oil for a leftover feast.

savoy cabbage
with bacon and cream

1 bay leaf

1 Savoy cabbage, about 3 lb

2 tablespoons unsalted butter

1 tablespoon extra virgin olive oil

4 oz thin bacon, chopped

a fresh sage sprig, leaves stripped and thinly sliced

¼ cup sour cream or heavy cream

sea salt and freshly ground black pepper

serves 4

Bring a large saucepan of water to a boil with the bay leaf and a large pinch of salt. Quarter the cabbage and blanch in the boiling water for 2–3 minutes. Drain well.

Core the cabbage quarters, then slice crosswise.

Heat the butter and oil in a large skillet. Add the bacon and sage and cook over high heat, stirring often, for 1 minute. Add the cabbage along with a pinch of salt and cook, stirring often, for 2–3 minutes.

Stir in the cream and cook until warmed through, about 1 minute. Season well and serve hot.

An ideal—and healthy—accompaniment to most roast meats, this dish is especially versatile because it can be made with baby chard, baby spinach, baby greens, or arugula. Simply use whatever happens to be in season. Use one of the suggested methods below, whichever suits you best.

wilted greens

1½ lb greens, mixed or single, such as baby chard, spinach, or arugula

extra virgin olive oil

1 lemon

1 garlic clove, peeled (Method two)

fine sea salt and freshly ground black pepper

serves 2–4

Method one (best for larger, robust greens, such as baby chard):
Bring a large saucepan of water to a boil. Salt well, add the greens, and blanch for 2–3 minutes. Drain and refresh under cold running water. Leave to dry in a colander, tossing occasionally to let all the water escape (squeeze excess with your hands if necessary). To serve, sprinkle with 2–3 tablespoons olive oil, the juice of ½ lemon, and a good sprinkling of salt and pepper.

Method two (best for smaller leaves, such as baby spinach, arugula, and mixed baby greens):
Crush the garlic clove, but leave whole and spear on the end of a fork. Heat about 2 tablespoons olive oil in a large pan. Add a very large handful of leaves and cook, stirring with the garlic fork, until wilted. Using tongs, transfer the leaves to a large plate and continue adding handfuls until all the greens are wilted. Season with a trickle of extra oil, a squeeze of lemon juice, and a good sprinkling of salt and pepper.

1 cup plus 1 tablespoon milk

2 large eggs

¾ cup all-purpose flour

½ teaspoon salt

4–6 tablespoons fat from the roasting pan

a small roasting pan, 18 x 12 inches, a 6-cup muffin pan, or a 12-cup pan

serves 6

horseradish sauce

1 large horseradish root

1 tablespoon white wine vinegar

1 cup heavy cream

sea salt

makes about 2 cups

Yorkshire pudding used to be served at the beginning of the meal to fill people up and make the meat "go further." These days, it acts as a mop for the gravy and pan juices. If you're lucky enough to have leftovers, they are delicious next day with bacon for breakfast. Fresh horseradish sauce is an eye-opener in more ways than one. Once you've made it yourself, the store-bought variety will never be good enough. Grating horseradish will make your eyes water, but the result is worth it.

yorkshire puddings
and horseradish sauce

Preheat the oven to 450°F.

Put the milk, eggs, flour, and salt in a bowl and beat well.

Heat the fat on top of the stove in one large pan or divide between a 6-cup pan (1 tablespoon fat for each cup) or a 12-cup pan (½ teaspoon fat for each cup). Pour in the batter (take care because it will spatter). Cook in the oven until well risen (35 minutes for the large pan or 15 minutes for the individual pans). Serve as soon as possible.

To make the horseradish sauce, scrape the fresh horseradish root clean and grate it finely to give 2 tablespoons. Put in a bowl, add the vinegar and salt, and stir well. Add the cream and beat until it becomes thick and light. Rest it at room temperature for at least 2 hours, but serve the same day.

desserts

Bread and butter pudding is a childhood favorite for many people, and is enjoying something of a revival at the moment. This version is made with brioche bread, in individual dishes, and cooks in under 20 minutes.

bread and butter puddings

1¼ cups milk

1¼ cups heavy cream

½ teaspoon vanilla essence

¼ cup sugar

3 eggs

6 thick slices of brioche bread or hot cross buns, about 8 oz, halved

⅓ cup golden raisins

1 whole nutmeg

6 individual dishes, 1 cup each, well greased

serves 6

Preheat the oven to 350°F.

Put the milk, cream, vanilla essence, and 3 tablespoons of the sugar into a saucepan and heat until the sugar dissolves.

Put the eggs into a bowl, beat well, stir in 2–3 tablespoons of the hot milk mixture to warm the eggs, then stir in the remainder of the hot milk.

Lightly toast the slices of brioche and cut into quarters. Divide between the prepared dishes and sprinkle with the golden raisins.

Pour in the custard, grate a little nutmeg over the top, then sprinkle with the remaining sugar. Bake for 18–20 minutes, or until firm. Let cool a little, then serve warm.

A British summer classic useful for using up overripe berries and slightly stale bread. Now that frozen summer fruits are readily available in most supermarkets, you can enjoy this dessert all year round.

summer pudding

If you are using fresh fruit, lightly rinse and leave to dry. Put the berries, honey, red wine, ½ cup water, and the cinnamon stick in a saucepan and gently simmer over low heat for 5 minutes, until the berries are plump and slightly softened. Remove from the heat and let cool. Discard the cinnamon stick.

Cut 6 slices of bread into triangles and use them to line the base and sides of the bowl or mold. Overlap the bread so it completely covers the bowl, leaving no gaps. Reserve the remaining slices. Spoon a little of the berry juice evenly over the bread in the bowl to moisten it. Fill the bowl with the berries, using a slotted spoon. Pack the fruit down with the back of a spoon, taking care not to squash the fruit too much. Cut the remaining slices of bread into triangles. Put these on top of the fruit to make a lid. Reserve any remaining berry juice.

Cover the bowl with plastic wrap, put a small plate on top, then put weights on the plate to press it down. Refrigerate overnight.

Remove the weights, plate, and plastic wrap. Put a plate upside down on top of the bowl. Invert the bowl and plate, then gently remove the bowl.

Put the reserved juice in a saucepan and heat gently. If necessary, gently drizzle the sauce over any parts of the pudding that are not a consistent color. Blend the arrowroot, if using, with 1 tablespoon of water and stir into the hot juice. Keep stirring until the juice thickens and clears. Pour the sauce over the pudding.

1 lb fresh or frozen berries, such as raspberries, blackberries, mulberries, or mixed summer berries, thawed, if frozen

2 tablespoons honey

½ cup red wine

1 cinnamon stick, bruised

8 slices of multi-grain day-old bread, crusts removed

1 teaspoon arrowroot (optional)

a 2-cup bowl or mold

serves 4

This is a very simple, classic recipe and there are hundreds of versions. Some cook on top of the stove, some call for long-grain rice, some add eggs or egg yolks, and some add flavorings such as orange peel or cinnamon. The list of things to serve with it is unlimited. Cooked and puréed apples or apricots, chocolate sauce, and custard are some traditional favorites.

rice pudding

½ cup risotto rice, such as arborio

2 cups whole milk, boiled

⅓ cup sugar

1 vanilla bean, split lengthwise with a small sharp knife

1 tablespoon unsalted butter

a pinch of salt

serves 4

Preheat the oven to 350°F.

Put the rice in a saucepan with a lid and add cold water to cover. Slowly bring to a boil over medium heat, then boil for 5 minutes. Drain the rice and rinse under cold water. Set aside to drain well.

Meanwhile, put the milk in an ovenproof pan with a lid and bring to a boil. Add the sugar and vanilla bean. Remove from the heat, cover, and let stand for 15 minutes. Using the tip of the knife, scrape out the vanilla seeds and stir them through the milk.

Add the rice to the milk, then add the butter and salt. Bring slowly to a boil. Cover and transfer to the oven. Do not stir. Cook until the rice is tender and the liquid is almost completely absorbed but not dry, about 25–35 minutes. Serve warm.

Simple to make yet stunningly beautiful. Choose well-shaped, ripe, but very firm pears, so they hold their form during cooking. They work well hot or cold, served with whipped cream studded with ginger and lemon peel.

pears in port
with juniper and ginger

8 firm pears, peeled and cored but left whole

1½ cups red wine

3 cups Ruby Port

1 tablespoon juniper berries, about 20 berries, crushed

peel of 1 unwaxed lemon, cut in a long strip

¼ cup sugar

3 pieces preserved stem ginger, finely diced, plus 2 tablespoons of the syrup

3 teaspoons arrowroot, blended with 2 tablespoons port

to serve

1 cup heavy cream, whipped to soft peaks

1 tablespoon syrup from the jar of preserved ginger

finely grated peel of ½ unwaxed lemon

serves 8

Preheat the oven to 300°F.

Stand the pears upright in a deep, ovenproof dish. Put the wine, port, juniper berries, lemon peel, and sugar in a saucepan and bring to a boil, stirring until the sugar dissolves. Pour the mixture over the pears to cover. Stir in the stem ginger and syrup.

Cover and bake for 45–60 minutes, or until the pears are very tender (depending on ripeness). Baste them 2–3 times during cooking.

Remove from the oven and, using a slotted spoon, transfer the pears to a deep bowl.

Pour the cooking liquid into a saucepan and stir in the blended arrowroot until mixed. Bring to a boil, stirring until the wine syrup is smooth and slightly thickened. Remove and discard the lemon peel, then pour the wine syrup over the pears. Serve immediately or refrigerate overnight: the pears will turn a deep purple-red and the spiced wine flavor will intensify dramatically.

To serve, mix the whipped cream, ginger syrup, and lemon peel until blended. Serve alongside the pears and drizzle over the wine syrup.

A simple dessert, but somehow deeply satisfying—maybe it's the butterscotch that makes it so irresistible. Since this is always a winner for people with a sweet tooth, make 2 extra apples, for seconds. The combination of dried fruit and cinnamon is reminiscent of Christmas.

4 tablespoons butter

3 tablespoons brown sugar

⅓ cup raisins

⅔ cup dried cranberries

⅔ cup dried cherries

6 cooking apples, cored

1 cinnamon stick, broken lengthwise into 6 thin strips

Butterscotch Sauce (page 164), warmed

an ovenproof dish, big enough to fit the apples, lightly greased

serves 4

baked stuffed apples
with butterscotch sauce

Preheat the oven to 375°F.

Put the butter and sugar into a bowl, beat until creamy, then stir in the dried fruits. Using a small, sharp knife, score the skin all the way around the middle of each apple, to prevent them bursting. Put the apples into the prepared dish, stuff with the dried fruit mixture, and put a piece of cinnamon into each. Bake on the middle shelf of the oven for 20 minutes, then reduce the temperature to 300°F and bake for a further 25 minutes, until soft and bubbling.

Serve the baked apples drizzled with the warmed Butterscotch Sauce.

Cranachan is a traditional Scottish dessert marrying oats, whisky, blackberries, and cream. It is an easy pudding to put together and chill ahead of time if necessary. This recipe also works well with raspberries or with a mixture of blueberries, blackberries, and strawberries. You can always use frozen mixed berries instead. You can also substitute any fruity alcoholic liqueur, such as peach schnapps, Grand Marnier, or Cointreau for the whisky.

blackberry cranachan

⅓ cup old-fashioned rolled oats

2 tablespoons soft brown sugar

⅔ cup extra thick cream

2 tablespoons whisky, plus extra to drizzle (optional)

½ lb blackberries

2 glasses, to serve

serves 2

Mix the oats and sugar together and spread them out on a baking sheet. Place the sheet under a medium-hot broiler. Cook until the sugar has caramelized, stirring the mixture from time to time. Remove from the broiler and set aside to cool.

Pour the cream into a large bowl, add the whisky, and stir until smooth. Loosely break up the cooled oat mixture between your fingers and add most of the crunchy oats to the cream, reserving a few tablespoons for the top.

Place some of the berries in the bottom of 2 glasses. Spoon a dollop of the cream over the top and then repeat the layers of fruit and cream a second time, finishing with the remaining blackberries.

To finish, sprinkle over the reserved oat mixture and drizzle with a little more whisky, if required.

4–5 medium cooking apples

½ lb fresh or frozen blackberries

¼ cup sugar

¼ teaspoon apple pie spice

finely grated peel and juice
of ½ unwaxed lemon

light cream or Real English Custard
(page 164), to serve

· **crumble topping**

1¾ sticks unsalted butter, chilled

1½ cups all-purpose flour

a pinch of salt

⅓ cup light brown or white sugar

a large, shallow, ovenproof dish

serves 6

Crumbles are quintessential British comfort food, best consumed on a miserable winter's night when you need warming up and comforting. If you are using frozen blackberries, there is no need to defrost them first. Bake the crumble in a moderate oven for a long time as this is what gives the topping its wonderful crunch.

classic blackberry and apple crumble

Preheat the oven to 350°F and set a baking sheet on the middle shelf to preheat.

Peel, core, and slice the apples and put them in a mixing bowl. Add the blackberries, sugar, apple pie spice, lemon peel, and juice and toss well to mix. Turn into the baking dish.

To make the crumble, rub the butter into the flour with the salt until it resembles rough bread crumbs. Alternatively, do this in a food processor. Stir in the sugar. (At this stage the mixture can be placed in a plastic bag and chilled in the fridge until ready to cook.) Lightly scatter the topping mixture over the apples and blackberries. Place on the baking sheet in the oven and bake for 50–60 minutes.

Remove from the oven and serve warm with light cream or the Real English Custard.

Summer has truly arrived when gooseberries become available. They seem to have a natural affinity with ginger. Try to track down some ginger wine as it is a delicious tipple and it really brings out the flavor of the gooseberries.

gooseberry and ginger wine crumble

2 lb green gooseberries, trimmed

3 tablespoons ginger wine

½ cup sugar

whipped cream, to serve

ginger topping

1½ cups all-purpose flour

1 teaspoon ground ginger

a pinch of salt

1 stick unsalted butter, chilled and cubed

½ cup sugar

a medium, shallow, ovenproof dish

serves 4

Preheat the oven to 375°F and set a baking sheet on the middle shelf to preheat.

Put the gooseberries in a non-reactive saucepan, add the ginger wine and sugar, and cook gently until the fruit starts to burst. Remove from the heat and tip the gooseberries into a strainer set over a clean pan to catch the juices. Next tip the gooseberries into the baking dish, covering the base with a single layer. Reserve the juices for later.

To make the ginger topping, put the flour, ginger, salt, and butter into a food processor and process until it looks like coarse bread crumbs. (Alternatively you can rub in by hand.) Tip into a mixing bowl and stir in the sugar.

Lightly sprinkle the topping mixture evenly over the prepared gooseberry mixture, mounding it up a little towards the center. Place the baking dish on top of the baking sheet in the oven and bake for about 25 minutes, until crisp and golden.

Remove from the oven and let cool for 5 minutes before serving with the warmed reserved juices and whipped cream.

Here's a traditional British childhood pudding, redolent of school dinners when it was invariably served with lumpy custard. This is a more sophisticated version, with orange to temper the sharp flavor of rhubarb.

rhubarb and orange crumble

Preheat the oven to 400°F and set a baking sheet on the middle shelf to preheat.

Trim the rhubarb, cut it into large chunks, and put in a large saucepan. Finely grate the peel from the oranges and add to the rhubarb. Stir in the ground ginger and sugar and cook over a gentle heat for a few minutes, stirring occasionally until the rhubarb begins to release its juices but is still holding its shape. Pour the rhubarb into a strainer set over a bowl to catch the juices and reserve these for later. Remove the pith from the oranges with a sharp knife then cut out the segments between the membrane. Add to the drained rhubarb and set aside to cool completely.

To make the almond topping, put the flour, salt, ground almonds, and butter in a food processor and process until it looks like coarse bread crumbs. (Alternatively you can rub in by hand.) Tip the mixture into a bowl and stir in the chopped nuts and sugar. (At this stage you can place it in a plastic bag and chill in the fridge until needed.)

Spoon the rhubarb and oranges into an ovenproof dish or 4 individual ones. Lightly sprinkle the almond mixture evenly over the surface, mounding it up a little towards the center. Place the baking dish on top of the baking sheet in the oven and bake for about 35 minutes, until crisp and golden.

Remove from the oven and let cool for 5 minutes before serving with heavy cream and the warmed reserved juices.

1½ lb fresh forced rhubarb (for its zing and color)

2 large unwaxed oranges

a pinch of ground ginger

¾ cup sugar

heavy cream, to serve

almond topping

1 cup all-purpose flour

a pinch of salt

⅔ cup ground almonds

1 stick unsalted butter, chilled

1 cup blanched almonds, chopped

¼ cup light brown sugar

a medium, shallow, ovenproof dish or 4 individual dishes

serves 4

Even if you never make desserts at any other time, you probably do when you have people to dinner. Perfect for such an occasion, these little plum fudge desserts can be prepared in advance, then cooked just before serving.

plum fudge puddings

4 tablespoons unsalted butter

4–5 tablespoons honey

2 tablespoons heavy cream

2 tablespoons brown sugar

1 teaspoon apple pie spice

1½ cups fresh white bread crumbs

2 ripe plums, halved, pitted, and thinly sliced

sour cream or crème fraîche, to serve

four ramekins, ⅔ cup each

serves 4

Preheat the oven to 400°F.

Put the butter, honey, and cream in a saucepan and heat until melted. Put the sugar, apple pie spice, and bread crumbs in a bowl and stir well.

Divide half the buttery fudge mixture between the ramekins and top with a layer of plum slices and half the bread crumb mix. Add the remaining plums and bread crumbs, then spoon over the remaining sauce.

Set on a baking sheet and bake for 20 minutes. Remove from the oven and let cool for 5 minutes, then carefully unmold the puddings and serve with a spoonful of sour cream or crème fraîche.

An individual white chocolate sponge dessert, baked with a hidden center of molten chocolate and served with cream, is perfect for any special occasion. It is very important to use the best-quality white and dark chocolate you can find.

light cream, to serve

dark chocolate filling

3 oz bittersweet chocolate, chopped

⅓ cup heavy cream

white chocolate sponge

3½ oz white chocolate, chopped

1½ sticks unsalted butter, at room temperature

¾ cup sugar

3 large eggs, beaten

1⅔ cup self-rising flour

a pinch of salt

½ teaspoon vanilla essence

about ¼ cup milk

an ice cube tray, oiled

6 small dessert molds, 2¾ inches diameter, well greased

serves 6

white and black desserts

The chocolate filling should be made at least 1 hour before making the sponge (though the filling can be kept in the freezer for up to 1 week). Put the chocolate in a heatproof bowl set over a pan of simmering water and melt gently (do not let the base of the bowl touch the water). Remove the bowl from the heat and stir until just smooth. Stir in the cream, then pour into the ice cube tray to make 6 "cubes." Freeze for at least 1 hour.

Preheat the oven to 350°F.

When you are ready to make the pudding, melt the white chocolate as above. When melted and smooth, let cool.

Put the butter in a bowl and beat the butter until creamy, then gradually beat in the sugar. When the mixture is very light and fluffy, beat in the eggs 1 tablespoon at a time, beating well after each addition. Using a large metal spoon, carefully fold in the flour and salt, then the melted chocolate, vanilla essence, and just enough milk to give the mixture a firm dropping consistency. Spoon into the prepared molds to fill by about half. Turn out the dark chocolate cubes, put one into the center of each mould, then fill with more sponge mixture to three-quarters full.

Stand the molds in a roasting pan, cover loosely with well-buttered aluminum foil, and bake for 25 minutes, or until just firm to the touch. Run a round-bladed knife inside each mold to loosen the puddings, then carefully turn out onto individual plates. Serve with cream.

A really popular sticky pudding from the Lake District of northern England that is just perfect for a cold day. The toffee sauce is also good with ice cream.

sticky toffee pudding

pudding

1 cup pitted chopped dates

1¼ cups boiling water

1 teaspoon baking soda

4 tablespoons unsalted butter, softened

¾ cup sugar

½ teaspoon vanilla essence

2 large eggs, at room temperature, beaten

1⅔ cups all-purpose flour

1 teaspoon baking powder

toffee sauce

⅔ cup packed soft dark brown sugar

4 tablespoons unsalted butter

1 cup light cream

an ovenproof baking dish, about 3 pints capacity, greased

makes 1 large pudding

Preheat the oven to 350°F.

To make the pudding, put the dates and the boiling water in a small saucepan or heatproof bowl, then stir in the baking soda and let soak until needed.

Put the butter in a mixing bowl or the bowl of an electric mixer. Add the sugar and vanilla essence and beat until very well combined (the mixture won't look soft and fluffy like a sponge cake mix).

Pour a little of the eggs into the mixing bowl and beat well. Keep on adding the eggs, a little at a time, then beating well, until all the eggs have been used up.

Sift the flour and baking powder into the bowl. Stir gently a few times to half-mix in the flour, then pour the date and water mixture into the bowl. Carefully mix the whole lot together to make a runny batter.

Pour the batter into the prepared baking dish and bake for about 40–45 minutes, or until golden brown. A skewer inserted into the center should come out clean. If not, give the pudding another 5 minutes in the oven before testing again.

While the pudding is baking, make the toffee sauce. Put the sugar, butter, and cream in a small saucepan. Set the pan over low heat and heat gently, stirring now and then until melted, smooth, and hot.

Remove the pudding from the oven and serve warm with the hot toffee sauce. Any leftover pudding and sauce can be gently reheated and served again. Eat within 2 days.

desserts
150

A simple cheesecake but all the better for it. The cottage cheese makes it light and fluffy so everyone will be coming back for seconds.

yorkshire cheesecake

7 oz ready-made shortcrust dough

8 oz cottage cheese

2 tablespoons sugar

2 eggs

finely grated peel of
1½ unwaxed lemons

freshly squeezed juice of ½ lemon

2 teaspoons cornstarch

2 tablespoons heavy cream

1 tablespoon butter, melted

2 oz raisins or currants, soaked in
boiling water for 20 minutes

*a deep pie plate or loose-based
tart pan, 10 inches diameter*

baking beans (optional)

serves 6

Preheat the oven to 400°F.

Roll out the dough thinly on a lightly floured work surface and use to line the pie plate or tart pan, then chill or freeze for 20 minutes. If using a pie plate, make a decorative edge. Cut out a piece of parchment paper to fit the plate or pan and use to line the pie crust, then fill with baking beans (or rice if you don't have baking beans). Bake for 10 minutes. Remove the parchment paper and beans and return to the oven for a further 5 minutes. Reduce the oven temperature to 350°F.

Press the cottage cheese through a fine-meshed strainer into a large bowl. Add the sugar, eggs, lemon peel, and juice and, using a wooden spoon or electric hand mixer, beat until smooth. Put the cornstarch and cream in another bowl, mix to a smooth paste, then beat into the cheese mixture with the melted butter. Pour the mixture into the pie crust.

Drain the raisins, pat dry with paper towels, then sprinkle them over the top of the cheesecake. Bake for 30 minutes, or until set. Let cool and serve at cool room temperature.

5 cooking apples

freshly squeezed juice of 1 lemon

1 cup sugar, plus extra to serve

2 teaspoons ground cinnamon

4 whole cloves

milk, to glaze

vanilla ice cream or light cream,
to serve

pie crust

2¼ cups all-purpose flour, sifted,
plus extra to dust

a pinch of salt

1½ sticks unsalted butter,
chilled and cubed

*a metal pie plate,
9 inches diameter*

serves 4–6

This is such a classic that it barely needs an introduction.
Everyone loves apple pie, and cloves and cinnamon
elevate this one to another level.

classic apple pie

To make the dough, put the flour and salt into a large bowl. Working
lightly, rub in the butter with your fingertips until the mixture resembles
bread crumbs. Alternatively, use a food processor. Add just enough cold
water (about 3–4 tablespoons) to bring the dough together. Gently form
into a ball, wrap in plastic wrap, and refrigerate for 20 minutes.

Preheat the oven to 425°F.

Remove the dough from the refrigerator and divide into 2 balls, one
slightly larger than the other. Put the larger piece of dough onto a lightly
floured surface and, using a rolling pin, gently flatten it out into a round.
Roll out and use to line the pie plate, leaving about 1 inch overhang.
Prick the base all over with a fork.

Peel, core, and slice the apples into a bowl, tossing them in lemon juice
to stop them discoloring. Mix the sugar and cinnamon in a bowl, then
put half the apples into the pie plate and sprinkle half the sugar and
cinnamon mixture over the top. Arrange the remaining apples on top and
sprinkle with the remaining sugar and cinnamon. Dot the cloves on top.

Roll out the remaining dough and use to cover the pie. Crimp the edges
to seal and trim off any excess. Pierce the lid and glaze with a little milk.

Bake for 15 minutes, then reduce the temperature to 350°F and bake
for a further 25–30 minutes, or until the pastry is golden brown and the
apples are well cooked. Sprinkle with extra sugar and serve hot with
vanilla ice cream or light cream.

A lovely dessert that's quick to make—but remember that it needs 3 hours in the fridge to set. It's pretty, tasty, and healthy too, so no need to feel guilty!

cranberry and raspberry jellies

1 tablespoon powdered gelatin

2 cups cranberry juice

1½ tablespoons sugar

8 cloves

1 cinnamon stick

6 slices of fresh ginger

1 cup fresh or frozen raspberries

serves 4

Sprinkle the gelatin over ½ cup of the cranberry juice and set aside.

Put the remaining cranberry juice, sugar, and spices in a saucepan and bring to a boil. Simmer gently for 2–3 minutes, then remove from the heat. Stir in the gelatin mixture, then set aside to cool.

Divide the raspberries between 4 glasses and strain the cooled jelly on top. Cover with plastic wrap and refrigerate for about 3 hours, or until set and ready to serve.

Syllabub—a velvety-smooth concoction of sweet wine and cream—is one of the great English desserts, dating from the sixteenth century. This one is made with orange rather than traditional lemon and topped with an irresistibly crunchy mixture of orange peel and sugar.

orange syllabub
with crunchy orange sprinkle

⅔ cup southern French Muscat or other strong sweet white wine (15 per cent ABV)

1 tablespoon Cointreau or other orange liqueur

finely grated peel of 2 unwaxed oranges

2 tablespoons freshly squeezed orange juice

2 tablespoons freshly squeezed lemon juice

4 tablespoons sugar

1¾ cups heavy cream, chilled

1 large bowl, chilled for 30–40 minutes in the refrigerator

6 glass dishes

serves 6

Pour the wine into a bowl, add the Cointreau, half the grated orange peel, the orange and lemon juice, and 2 tablespoons of the sugar. Stir, cover, and refrigerate for several hours or overnight.

Mix the remaining orange peel and sugar in a bowl. Spread it over a plate and leave for a couple of hours to crisp up. Store it in an airtight container until ready to use.

Strain the wine mixture through a fine-meshed, nonmetal strainer. Pour the cream into the large chilled bowl and beat with an electric mixer until it starts to thicken. Gradually add the orange-flavored wine, beating well after each addition until the cream thickens again—you want a thick pouring consistency. When the final addition of wine has been incorporated the mixture should hold a trail when you lift out the beaters, but it shouldn't be stiff. (Don't overbeat it, or it will separate.) Ladle the mixture into the 6 glass dishes and refrigerate for at least 1 hour before serving.

Serve sprinkled with the crunchy orange sprinkle.

Ladyfingers soaked in sherry and topped with fruit, homemade egg custard, and cream, create this delicious trifle, which is ideal for an alternative Christmas dessert. Try canned apricots instead of peaches or 12–14 oz thinly sliced Madeira cake instead of the ladyfingers.

old english trifle

12 ladyfingers

½ cup raspberry jam

4½ oz amaretti, lightly crushed

15 oz canned peach slices in fruit juice

6 tablespoons sherry

1 tablespoon cornstarch

2⅓ cups whole milk

4 egg yolks

¼ cup sugar

1 teaspoon vanilla essence

1¼ cups heavy cream

⅓ cup toasted slivered almonds

a *deep glass serving bowl*

serves 8

Spread the top of each ladyfinger with jam, then arrange them in the base of the serving bowl, covering the base completely. Sprinkle the crushed amaretti evenly over the top.

Drain the peaches, reserving the juice. Mix together the peach juice and sherry, then pour evenly over the ladyfingers and amaretii. Arrange the peaches in an even layer over the top. Cover and refrigerate.

Meanwhile, put the cornstarch in a heatproof bowl, add 3 tablespoons of the milk, and blend together with a whisk until smooth. Add the egg yolks, sugar, and vanilla essence and beat together to mix. Set aside.

Pour the remaining milk in a saucepan and heat gently until almost boiling. Pour the hot milk onto the egg yolk mixture, beating constantly. Return the mixture to the pan, then cook gently, stirring continuously, until the mixture thickens enough to coat the back of a wooden spoon. Do not allow the mixture to boil as it may curdle.

Remove the pan from the heat and pour the custard into a heatproof bowl. Cover the surface of the hot custard with a piece of parchment paper (to prevent a skin forming) and set aside to cool completely.

Spoon the cold custard over the peach layer. Lightly whip the cream until it forms soft peaks, then spread over the custard, covering it completely. Cover and refrigerate for 3–4 hours before serving. Sprinkle the cream with the slivered almonds, then serve.

2 cups fresh white bread crumbs

½ cup all-purpose flour

7 oz shredded suet

1 cup packed light brown sugar

1½ teaspoons apple pie spice

1⅓ cups golden raisins

1⅓ cups currants

⅓ cup candied peel or raisins

½ cup slivered or chopped almonds

finely grated peel of 1 unwaxed lemon

1 cooking apple, peeled, cored, and grated

4 eggs, beaten

3 tablespoons brandy, rum, or sherry

freshly squeezed lemon juice or milk (optional)

brandy butter

1 stick unsalted butter, softened

½ cup packed light brown sugar

5–6 tablespoons brandy

a 1.5-quart heatproof ceramic pudding bowl, greased and base-lined with nonstick baking parchment

kitchen twine

serves 8

A British Christmas wouldn't be the same without a homemade Christmas pudding. Lovingly prepared up to 8 weeks in advance, it's a boozy dessert best served with lashings of heartstopping brandy butter.

traditional christmas pudding

Put the bread crumbs, flour, suet, sugar, apple pie spice, golden raisins, currants, candied peel, almonds, lemon peel, and apple in a large bowl and stir until well mixed. Add the eggs and brandy and mix thoroughly, adding a little lemon juice to moisten the mixture, if necessary.

Fill the prepared bowl with the mixture, pressing down well. Cover the pudding with a disk of parchment paper, then cover the basin with parchment paper and aluminum foil, pleat them in the center, then secure under the rim with twine.

Put the bowl in the top of a steamer. Steam the pudding over a pan of gently simmering water for 5–6 hours, topping up with boiling water periodically so that the pan doesn't boil dry. Remove the pudding from the steamer and set aside to cool. Once cold, re-cover with parchment paper and foil, and store in a cool, dry, dark place for 6–8 weeks.

On Christmas Day, steam the pudding, as before, for 3–4 hours.

To make the brandy butter, put the butter in a bowl and beat with a wooden spoon until it is very soft and creamy. Gradually beat in the sugar until the mixture is very light and fluffy, then beat in the brandy, 1 tablespoon at a time, until well combined. Transfer the mixture to a serving bowl, cover, and refrigerate for at least 2–3 hours before serving.

Invert the pudding onto a warmed plate and serve with brandy butter.

This makes a deliciously sticky pouring sauce. For a variation, simply stir in ⅓ cup finely chopped stem ginger.

butterscotch sauce

½ stick unsalted butter

⅓ cup light brown sugar

¼ cup sugar

½ cup corn syrup

1¼ cups heavy cream

½ teaspoon vanilla essence

serves 4–6

Put the butter, light brown sugar, sugar, and corn syrup in a pan. Stir over low heat until the sugars have dissolved and then bubble gently for 5 minutes, until smooth and thick.

Remove the pan from the heat and stir in the heavy cream and vanilla essence. Keep warm if using immediately.

There will be more than enough sauce for four servings but it will keep in the fridge for up to a week. Just reheat gently to serve.

This classic creamy sauce is a staple of English cooking— pour generously over crumbles, pies, and fruit.

real english custard

1 vanilla bean, split lengthwise

1¼ cups whole milk

2 egg yolks

1–2 tablespoons superfine sugar

serves 4

Scrape out the seeds from the vanilla bean and reserve. Put the milk, vanilla seeds, and vanilla bean in a pan. Bring to boiling point, then turn off the heat and infuse for 15 minutes. Remove the vanilla bean.

Put the egg yolks and sugar in a bowl and beat until pale. Pour over the infused milk, mix well, and return to the pan. Stir with a wooden spoon over very gentle heat until the custard thickens enough to coat the back of the spoon. Do not allow to overheat or it will curdle.

Use immediately or cover the surface directly with plastic wrap, set aside to cool, then chill. Reheat very gently before serving.

breads

This loaf has a moist, chewy crumb and a good crunchy crust, and baking it will fill the house with a most wonderful smell. It's a real treat!

old-fashioned cottage loaf

4²⁄₃ cups all-purpose flour

2 teaspoons sea salt

2 tablespoons unsalted butter, cubed

a 0.6-oz cake compressed yeast*

1 rounded teaspoon honey

450 ml tepid water

1 egg, beaten, to glaze

a large baking sheet, greased

makes 1 large loaf

*To use active dry yeast, mix one ¹⁄₄-oz package with the flour and butter mixture, then add the honey and tepid water and mix as in the main recipe.

Mix the flour and salt in a bowl. Add the butter and rub in with your fingertips until the mixture looks like crumbs. Make a well in the center.

Crumble the yeast into a bowl, add the honey and a quarter of the water, then stir until smooth and creamy. Pour the mixture into the well, then add the remaining water. Gradually work the flour into the liquid to make a slightly firm dough. If the dough feels sticky or soft, work in extra flour, 1 tablespoon at a time. Turn out onto a lightly floured work surface and knead for 10 minutes until the dough feels very pliable and smooth.

Return the dough to the bowl, cover with plastic wrap, and let rise at room temperature until doubled in size, about 1¹⁄₂–2 hours.

Turn out onto a lightly floured work surface and punch down. Cut off one-third of the dough, then gently shape both pieces into balls. Put, well apart, on a well-floured work surface, covered with a sheet of plastic wrap, then leave until almost doubled in size, about 45–60 minutes.

Preheat the oven to 450°F.

Lift the larger ball onto the baking sheet and flatten it slightly. Flatten the smaller ball and set it on top. Push 2 fingers and a thumb joined together down into the middle of the loaf to press both pieces together. Leave for about 5–10 minutes, then glaze with the beaten egg. Using a small sharp knife, score all around the edge of both balls.

Bake for 15 minutes, then reduce the temperature to 400°F and bake for 20 minutes, or until the loaf sounds hollow when tapped underneath.

This is the classic Irish soda bread made with baking soda as the raising agent rather than yeast. This means that the dough can be baked immediately, rather than having to let it rise as with a yeasted dough. Quick and easy to make.

soda bread

2⅔ cups whole wheat flour, plus extra to dust

1 teaspoon baking soda

1 teaspoon salt

1 teaspoon sugar

1¼ cups buttermilk

makes 1 small loaf

Preheat the oven to 450°F.

Put the flour, baking soda, salt, and sugar into a bowl and mix well. Make a well in the center, add the buttermilk, and gradually work it into the flour to make a soft dough.

Knead on a lightly floured surface for 5 minutes and then shape into a flattened round loaf. Transfer to a greased baking sheet and, using a sharp knife, cut a cross in the top of the dough. Dust with a little extra flour.

Bake for 15 minutes, then reduce the temperature to 400°F and bake for a further 30 minutes, or until risen and the loaf sounds hollow when tapped underneath.

Transfer to a wire rack and let cool completely.

A quick, simple bread that's perfect for serving alongside a cheese board. This bread goes well with all kinds of cheeses, especially young goat cheese, Cheddar-style cheeses, and creamy blues.

raisin and rosemary bread

1¾ cups white bread flour, plus extra to dust

1 cup whole-wheat flour

¾ cups rye flour

1½ teaspoons fast-action yeast

1½ teaspoons fine sea salt

1 tablespoon finely chopped fresh rosemary leaves plus 2 extra sprigs for topping

1 tablespoon soft brown sugar

1½ cups tepid water

2 tablespoons olive oil

½ cup raisins

makes 1 medium loaf

Put the white, whole-wheat, and rye flours in a large bowl and mix. Add the yeast, sea salt, and rosemary and stir. Dissolve the sugar in 2 tablespoons of the water. Make a well in the flour and pour in the dissolved sugar and olive oil, followed by the remaining water. Start working the flour into the liquid with a wooden spoon then mix with your hands until all the flour is incorporated.

Turn the dough onto a lightly floured work surface and knead for 5 minutes, or until the dough begins to feel elastic. Flatten the dough and add half the raisins. Fold over and knead for a couple of seconds, then repeat with the remaining raisins. Carry on kneading for a further 5 minutes. Put the dough in a large bowl, cover with a slightly damp kitchen towel and leave for 45–50 minutes, or until doubled in size.

Turn out the dough and punch down. Roll up into a sausage shape and tuck in the ends. Put on a greased baking sheet, make 3 or 4 diagonal cuts in the dough with a sharp knife, cover with the damp kitchen towel and leave for a further 25 minutes.

Preheat the oven to 400°F.

Brush the top of the loaf lightly with water and scatter the remaining rosemary leaves on top, pressing them lightly into the dough. Bake for 35–40 minutes, or until the loaf is brown and sounds hollow when tapped on the base. Let cool on a wire rack for at least 45 minutes before serving.

2 tablespoons unsalted butter

1 large leek, trimmed and finely chopped, about 5 oz prepared weight

a good pinch of dried sage or 1 teaspoon chopped fresh sage (optional)

freshly ground black pepper

1⅔ cups all-purpose flour

1⅔ cups stone-ground whole-wheat flour

1½ teaspoons sea salt

1 cup tepid milk mixed with 1 cup tepid water

a 0.6-oz cake compressed yeast*

1 cup Asiago cheese

to glaze

3 tablespoons milk mixed with a good pinch of salt

cracked wheat berries or oatmeal, to sprinkle

2 baking sheets, greased

makes 2 round loaves

*To use active dry yeast, mix one ¼-oz package with the flours and salt, then add the milk and water mixture and continue as in the main recipe.

Bread flavored with leeks or onions plus cheese and sage is commonly found in Wales and west England.

cheese and leek bread

Melt the butter in a skillet. Add the leek, sage, and pepper and cook slowly, stirring occasionally, until softened. Cool until just warm.

Mix the flours and salt in a large bowl, then make a well in the center. Put the milk-water mixture into a bowl, crumble the yeast over the top, and stir until completely dispersed. Pour into the well, then gradually work in the flour to make a soft dough. If the dough feels sticky, work in a little more flour, 1 tablespoon at a time: if the dough feels tough and dry, work in a little more tepid milk or water, 1 tablespoon at a time.

Turn out the dough on a lightly floured work surface and knead for 10 minutes, or until very pliable. Gently work in the leek mixture until thoroughly mixed, then flatten the dough until it is about 1 inch thick. Crumble the cheese onto the dough. Cut the dough into three equal pieces and stack them together, pressing down well. Cut the stack in half, then put one piece on top of the other and press down. Return the dough to the bowl, cover with plastic wrap, then let rise in a warm place until doubled in size, about 1 hour.

Turn out onto a lightly floured work surface and punch down. Divide into two 6-inch disks. Set on the prepared sheets, then put in a large plastic bag and inflate slightly. Let rise as before until almost doubled in size, about 45 minutes. Preheat the oven to 425°F.

Uncover the loaves and brush lightly with the milk-salt mixture. Sprinkle with cracked wheat berries. Bake for 25 minutes, or until they are golden brown and sound hollow when tapped underneath. Cool slightly on a wire rack. Eat while still warm.

Bread made with a good proportion of cooled mashed potatoes has a wonderful flavor, excellent light texture, and lots of nutritional value. Popular with Irish settlers in America, Australia, and New Zealand, this bread is well worth adding to your repertoire. Use baking potatoes in the ratio of four parts flour to one part mashed potato.

potato bread rolls

5¾ cups all-purpose flour

4 tablespoons unsalted butter, cubed

1 tablespoon sea salt

1 cup cooled mashed potatoes

1⅔ cups tepid milk

a 0.6-oz cake compressed yeast*

2 baking sheets, greased

makes 18 rolls

*To use active dry yeast, mix one ¼-oz package with the flour, then rub in the butter, mix in the salt and potato, and bind to a dough with the milk.

Put the flour in a large mixing bowl, add the butter, and rub in with your fingertips until the mixture looks like fine crumbs. Stir in the salt and mashed potatoes.

Put the milk in a measuring cup, crumble the yeast over the top, and stir well until dispersed. Pour onto the flour mixture and mix to make a firm dough.

Turn out onto a floured work surface and knead for 10 minutes. Return the dough to the bowl, cover with plastic wrap, and let rise in a warm place until doubled in size, about 1½ hours.

Turn out the risen dough and punch down. Divide the dough into 18 equal pieces. Arrange on the prepared baking sheets, then slip them into 2 large plastic bags and let rise as before until doubled in size, about 30 minutes.

Preheat the oven to 425°F.

Uncover the loaves and bake for 15–20 minutes, or until they sound hollow when tapped underneath. Cool on a wire rack.

Crisp, crumbly Scottish oatcakes have been made for centuries and are still very popular. They are good with soft cheeses or strong Cheddars, or spread with butter and jam or honey. This recipe uses olive oil rather than the traditional lard, as well as fine oatmeal, available from natural food stores.

oatcakes

1⅓ cups fine oatmeal, plus extra for rolling out

½ teaspoon sea salt

2 pinches of baking powder

3 tablespoons olive oil

½ cup minus 1 tablespoon boiling water

a 2½-inch cookie cutter

several baking sheets, greased

makes about 16 oatcakes

Preheat the oven to 325°F.

Put the oatmeal, salt, baking powder, and olive oil in a food processor. With the motor running, pour in the boiling water through the feed tube. Process until the mixture just comes together. Remove the dough from the processor and put onto a work surface sprinkled with oatmeal. If the dough is very sticky, work in a little extra oatmeal—the dough soon firms up. Roll out the dough to about ¼ inch thick, then cut out rounds using the cookie cutter. Knead the trimmings together, then re-roll and cut out more rounds. Arrange the oatcakes slightly apart on the prepared sheets and bake for about 15 minutes, or until the edges are light brown.

Let cool on the baking sheets for 2 minutes, then transfer to a wire rack to cool completely.

If the oatcakes become soft, they can be crisped up in the oven (heated as above) for 5 minutes.

variations At the same time as the oatmeal, add either:
• 3 pinches of hot red pepper flakes to make spicy oatcakes
• 4 teaspoons poppy seeds or sesame seeds
• 1 tablespoon fresh thyme leaves

teatime

Often referred to as Gentleman's Relish, there's something quintessentially English about anchovy relish spread on crisp little toasts. These sophisticated bites make a wonderful start to afternoon tea, especially when served with a light, refreshing cup of Earl Grey or Darjeeling. Leftover relish can be stored in the refrigerator for several days.

little toasts with anchovy butter

3 oz canned anchovy fillets, about 8, drained

¼ cup milk

4 tablespoons unsalted butter

a pinch of cayenne pepper

a pinch of ground nutmeg

a pinch of ground coriander

¼ teaspoon freshly squeezed lemon juice

8 quails' eggs

4 wafer-thin slices of whole-wheat bread

2–3 tablespoons chopped fresh flatleaf parsley

freshly ground black pepper

makes 16 toasts

Soak the anchovy fillets in the milk for about 10 minutes.

Drain the anchovy fillets and put them in a food processor with the butter, cayenne pepper, nutmeg, coriander, lemon juice, and a good grinding of black pepper. Process until smooth and creamy.

Bring a saucepan of water to a boil, add the quails' eggs, then reduce the heat and simmer for about 4 minutes. Drain, then cover in cold water and let cool.

To serve, peel the eggs and cut in half lengthwise. Toast the slices of bread until crisp and golden. Cut off and discard the crusts, then cut into quarters. Spread with a thin layer of anchovy relish, top with half a quail's egg, and sprinkle with a little parsley. Serve immediately.

Savory scones filled with cream cheese and peppery watercress, or topped with sweet juicy grapes, make a wonderful alternative to the classic sweet Scones with Clotted Cream and Strawberry Jam (page 203). They are just a few mouthfuls each, so you'll still have plenty of room for a few cakes and fancies.

baby cheese scones

$1\frac{3}{4}$ cups all-purpose flour

4 teaspoons baking powder

a pinch of salt

$\frac{1}{4}$ teaspoon freshly ground black pepper

3 tablespoons unsalted butter, chilled and cubed

$2\frac{1}{2}$ oz very sharp Cheddar cheese, grated

1 egg

$\frac{1}{3}$ cup plus 1 tablespoon milk

to serve

about 5 oz cream cheese

2 handfuls of watercress or 1 cup seedless grapes, halved

a $1\frac{3}{4}$-inch cookie cutter

makes 16 scones

Preheat the oven to 425°C.

Put the flour, baking powder, salt, and pepper in a food processor and pulse to combine. Add the butter and process for about 20 seconds until the mixture resembles fine bread crumbs. Transfer to a large bowl and stir in $\frac{1}{2}$ cup of the cheese, then make a well in the center of the mixture.

Beat together the egg and milk in another bowl, reserving 1 tablespoon of the mixture in a separate bowl. Pour most of the remaining liquid into the flour mixture and bring together into a soft dough using a fork. If there are still dry crumbs, add a little more of the liquid. Turn out onto a lightly floured surface and knead very briefly, then gently pat or roll out to about 1 inch thick. Cut out rounds with the cookie cutter, pressing the trimmings together to make more scones.

Arrange the scones on a greased baking sheet, spacing them slightly apart. Brush the tops with the reserved egg and milk mixture and sprinkle over the remaining cheese. Bake for about 10 minutes, or until risen and golden. Transfer to a wire rack and let cool.

To serve, split the scones and spread the bottom half with a thick layer of cream cheese, top with watercress, then finish with the scone lid. Alternatively, split the scones, spread each half with cream cheese, and top with halved grapes.

These were named after the maids of honor who carried them back to Richmond Palace for King Henry VIII or Queen Elizabeth I—both monarchs, it is said, loved these little cheesecakes made by a local baker. These include a spoonful of best cherry conserve in the base of each—almond and cherry make a great combination. Make these in small, deep pans if you can find them, as the filling seems moister and they look great!

little richmond maids of honor

14 oz ready-made sweet shortcrust pastry dough, at room temperature

8 sprigs of rosemary (optional)

confectioners' sugar, to dust

filling

½ stick unsalted butter

¼ cup plus 2 tablespoons sugar

finely grated peel and juice of 1 unwaxed lemon

½ cup cottage cheese

2 large eggs, beaten

⅓ cup brandy or cherry brandy

1 cup ground almonds

a pinch of salt

about ¾ cup cherry conserve

eight 4-inch false-bottom tartlet pans

makes 8 maids of honor

Roll out the dough thinly on a lightly floured work surface and use to line the tartlet pans. Set on a baking sheet and refrigerate for 30 minutes.

Preheat the oven to 350°F.

Put the butter, sugar, and lemon peel in a large bowl and beat until pale and fluffy. Press the cottage cheese through a fine-meshed strainer into another bowl (do not blend in a food processor, otherwise the texture will be altered), then beat the cottage cheese into the butter and sugar mixture. Beat in the eggs, lemon juice, and brandy, then gently fold in the ground almonds and a pinch of salt.

Drop a spoonful of cherry conserve in each cheesecake crust, then add the almond filling to about two-thirds full to leave room for rising. Bake for 20–25 minutes, or until risen and golden brown. Remove from the oven and let cool slightly. Spear each cheesecake with a sprig of fresh rosemary and serve warm, dusted with confectioners' sugar.

There's nothing quite as delicious as a real custard tart. The nutmeg is the classic flavoring here, but the milk is also infused with fresh bay leaves to add a mysterious musky scent to the custard. Fresh bay leaves should be more widely used in cooking—the flavor is like nutmeg, but "greener" and sweeter.

little nutmeg and bay leaf custard tarts

14 oz ready-made *pâte sucrée* or sweet shortcrust pastry dough, at room temperature

2⅔ cups whole milk

3 fresh (preferably) or dried bay leaves

6 egg yolks

⅓ cup sugar

1 whole nutmeg

eight 4-inch false-bottom tart pans (or use smaller but deeper pans and increase the cooking time)

makes about 8 tarts

Preheat the oven to 400°F and put a baking sheet on the middle shelf to preheat.

Roll out the dough thinly on a lightly floured work surface and use to line the tart pans. Put these on a baking sheet and refrigerate for 30 minutes.

Put the milk and bay leaves in a saucepan and heat until lukewarm. Put the egg yolks and sugar into a bowl and beat until pale and creamy. Pour the warmed milk onto the yolks and stir well—do not beat or you will get bubbles. Strain into a small pitcher and pour into the tart cases. Grate fresh nutmeg liberally over the surface of the tartlets.

Put the tart pans on the preheated sheet and bake for 10 minutes. Reduce the temperature to 350°F and bake until set and just golden—about 10 minutes. Don't overbake as the custard should be a bit wobbly when the tarts come out of the oven.

Remove from the pans and let cool on a wire rack. Serve warm.

Along with Traditional Christmas Pudding (see page 163), mincemeat pies are also an essential part of British yuletide festivities. To give the pies an extra Christmassy feel, cut the pastry lids into star shapes using a star-shaped cutter, rather than rounds.

mincemeat pies

1½ cups all-purpose flour

a pinch of salt

1 stick butter, chilled and cubed

8 oz mincemeat

milk, to glaze

sugar, to dust

whipped cream or Brandy Butter (page 163), to serve

a 3-inch fluted cookie cutter

a 2½-inch fluted cookie cutter

a 12-cup muffin pan, greased

makes 12 mincemeat pies

Sift the flour and salt in a bowl and add the butter. Using your fingertips, lightly rub the butter into the flour until the mixture resembles fine bread crumbs. Gradually add 3–4 tablespoons water, stirring with a blunt knife or a palette knife, until the mixture begins to come together in large lumps. Add a little extra water, if necessary.

Collect the dough together and knead it gently, very briefly, on a lightly floured surface. Wrap in plastic wrap and refrigerate for 30 minutes.

Preheat the oven to 375°F.

Roll out just over half the dough on a lightly floured surface and stamp out 12 circles of dough using the larger cutter. Gently press into the muffin pan. Divide the mincemeat evenly between the pie crusts.

Roll out the remaining dough and stamp out 12 circles using the smaller cutter. Dampen the edges of the dough circles with water, then place them on top of the mincemeat and dough in the muffin pan, dampened edges down. Press the edges together to seal. Glaze the tops of the pies with a little milk, then dust with sugar. Using a sharp knife, cut a slit in the top of each pie. Bake for 20–25 minutes, or until the dough is cooked and lightly browned.

Remove from the oven and leave the mincemeat pies in the pan for a couple of minutes, then transfer to a wire rack to cool. Serve warm with whipped cream or Brandy Butter.

Rich, traditional, and crumbly, these cookies were made to contrast with the privations of Lent, and echo the rich (and expensive) flavors of simnel cakes—dried fruit, butter, and spices or lemon.

easter cookies

1 stick unsalted butter, softened

⅓ cup sugar

1 egg yolk

finely grated peel of
1 unwaxed lemon

1½ cups all-purpose flour

a good pinch of baking powder

a pinch of salt

⅓ cup golden raisins

topping

1 egg white, lightly beaten

sugar, to dust

a 3-inch fluted cookie cutter

several baking sheets, greased

makes 16 cookies

Put the butter, sugar, and egg yolk in a bowl and beat until light and creamy. Beat in the lemon peel, then add the flour, baking powder, salt, and golden raisins. Mix with a wooden spoon. Bring the dough together with your hands. Wrap in plastic wrap and refrigerate until firm—about 20 minutes. At this point, the dough can be stored in the refrigerator for up to 3 days.

Preheat the oven to 400°F.

Roll out the dough on a floured work surface to about ¼ inch thick. Cut into rounds with the cookie cutter. Arrange well apart on the prepared baking sheets. Bake for about 10 minutes, or until pale golden and firm.

Remove the sheets from the oven and lightly glaze each cookie with beaten egg white, then dust with a little sugar. Return to the oven and bake for a further 3–5 minutes, or until the tops are golden and crunchy.

Remove from the oven and let cool on the sheets for a minute, then transfer to a wire rack to cool completely.

variation Omit the lemon peel. Add ½ teaspoon apple pie spice, ½ teaspoon ground cinnamon, and a good pinch of grated nutmeg to the flour. Use currants or raisins instead of the golden raisins, and add 1 teaspoon finely chopped mixed candied peel if you like.

Parkin is a kind of sticky gingerbread from Yorkshire, made with oatmeal, molasses, and spice. These cookies are made from the same ingredients and have the same flavor and a crunchy texture.

parkin cookies

¾ cup plus 2 tablespoons self-rising flour

¾ cup fine oatmeal

1 teaspoon ground ginger

½ teaspoon ground allspice

3 tablespoons dark brown sugar

6 tablespoons unsalted butter

2 tablespoons light corn syrup

1 tablespoon molasses

confectioners' sugar, to dust (optional)

several baking sheets, greased

makes 20 cookies

Preheat the oven to 350°F.

Put the flour, oatmeal, ginger, allspice, and sugar in a large bowl and mix thoroughly. Make a well in the center.

Put the butter, light corn syrup, and molasses in a small saucepan and heat gently until melted.

Pour the mixture into the well in the dry ingredients and mix well with a wooden spoon. Using floured hands, take walnut-size portions of the dough (about a tablespoon) and roll into balls. Set well apart on the prepared baking sheets. Bake for 15 minutes, or until firm.

Let cool on the sheets for 2 minutes to firm up, then transfer to a wire rack to cool completely. Serve dusted with confectioners' sugar, if using.

The better the butter you use here, the finer the flavor and texture—a salty, blended butter will make the shortbread heavier so use a good unsalted one. Shortbread can be cut into disks or pressed into a shallow cake pan to make thicker "petticoat tails."

scottish shortbread

2 cups all-purpose flour

⅓ cup rice flour, ground rice, or cornstarch

½ cup sugar, plus extra to dust

1¾ sticks unsalted butter, chilled and cubed

a 9-inch round cake pan, lightly greased, or a 3-inch fluted cookie cutter

several baking sheets, greased

makes about 20 rounds or 12 petticoat tails

Put the all-purpose flour, rice flour, and sugar in a food processor. Process until thoroughly mixed. Add the butter and process until everything comes together to make a ball of dough. Carefully remove from the machine.

If making petticoat tails, lightly flour your fingers, then gently press the dough into the cake pan to make an even layer. Prick the dough all over with a fork, then gently score into 12 segments using a sharp knife.

If making rounds, roll out the dough on a lightly floured work surface to about ¼ inch thick and cut out rounds with the cookie cutter. Knead the trimmings, then re-roll and cut out more rounds. Put the rounds slightly apart on the prepared baking sheets. Prick all over with a fork.

Preheat the oven to 350°F.

Refrigerate the shortbread for 15 minutes, then bake for 15–20 minutes for the petticoat tails and 10–12 minutes for the rounds, or until just firm and barely colored. Dust the shortbread with a little sugar, then let cool for 2 minutes. For petticoat tails, cut the segments along the marked lines, then leave until cold before removing from the pan. For the rounds, transfer to a wire rack to cool completely.

These are the stuff of childhood teatimes when you slathered butter on a piping hot crumpet and let the molten butter drip down your chin. They're just as good with jam or honey, and a steaming cup of tea.

crumpets

1¼ cups milk mixed with 1¼ cups water

a 0.6-oz cake compressed yeast*

3 cups all-purpose flour

½ teaspoon baking soda

1 teaspoon salt

to serve

unsalted butter

berry jam or honey

2–3 crumpet rings or cookie cutters

a flat griddle pan or skillet, preheated and greased

makes 12 crumpets

*To use active dry yeast, mix one ¼-oz package with the flour and continue as in the main recipe.

Warm the milk and water mixture in a small saucepan. If using fresh yeast, put it into a small bowl with a little of the warm liquid, stir well, then add the remaining milk and water. Sift the flour into a mixing bowl, then stir in the warm yeast mixture.

Cover the bowl with a clean kitchen towel and leave in a warm place for 1 hour.

Put the baking soda and salt into a bowl, add 2 tablespoons water, mix well, then beat it into the mixture. Set aside for a further 45 minutes.

Put the greased crumpet rings on the prepared griddle pan and set over medium heat. When the rings are hot, spoon 2 tablespoons of the batter into each ring—just enough to cover the base. Cook for 4–5 minutes, until the underside is golden, then remove the rings and turn the crumpet over to brown the top.

To serve, toast the crumpets on both sides, smother them with butter and stack on a hot plate. Serve with extra butter and a dish of berry jam or honey. A cup of tea is the traditional accompaniment.

Soft and spicy, and dripping with melted butter, nothing quite makes a teatime like hot buttered teacakes. These ones are small, rather than the traditional large ones, so there'll be plenty of room for those other teatime scones and sandwiches.

toasted teacakes

1¾ cups white bread flour

½ teaspoon salt

1 teaspoon easy-blend dry yeast

1½ tablespoons soft brown sugar

¼ teaspoon freshly grated nutmeg

⅓ cup mixed dried fruits

3 dried apricots, chopped

3 tablespoons butter

½ cup milk, plus extra to glaze

2 baking sheets, greased

makes 8 teacakes

Combine the flour, salt, yeast, sugar, and nutmeg in a bowl, then sift into a larger bowl. Stir in the dried fruits, then make a well in the center.

Melt the butter in a small saucepan, then add the milk and heat until lukewarm. Pour into the flour mixture, gradually working it in to make a soft dough. Turn out onto a lightly floured surface and knead for about 5 minutes, or until smooth and elastic. Transfer to a bowl, wrap in a plastic bag, and let rise in a warm place for about 1 hour, or until doubled in size.

Turn the dough out onto a lightly floured work surface, punch down, and divide into 8 equal pieces. Shape each one into a disk and arrange on the prepared baking sheets, spacing them slightly apart. Wrap the baking sheets in plastic bags and let rise as above for about 45 minutes, or until doubled in size.

Preheat the oven to 400°F.

Brush the teacakes with milk, then bake for about 15 minutes, or until risen and golden, and they sound hollow when tapped. Transfer to a wire rack to cool. To serve, cut the teacakes in half and toast, then spread generously with butter.

Traditionally served with clotted cream and rich, fruity jam, these classic scones are a must for the tea table. Originally made in Devon and Cornwall, clotted cream is formed by gently heating milk to produce a really rich, thick cream. However, if you can't get hold of any clotted cream, use whipped cream instead.

scones *with clotted cream and strawberry jam*

1¾ cups self-rising flour

1 teaspoon baking powder

2 tablespoons sugar

3 tablespoons unsalted butter, chilled and cubed

1 egg

⅓ cup milk

to serve

clotted cream

good-quality strawberry jam

a 2-inch cookie cutter

makes 10–12 scones

Preheat the oven to 425°F.

Put the flour, baking powder, and sugar in a food processor and pulse to combine. Add the butter and process for about 20 seconds until the mixture resembles fine bread crumbs. Transfer to a large bowl and make a well in the center.

Beat together the egg and milk in another bowl, reserving 1 tablespoon of the mixture in a separate bowl. Pour most of the remaining liquid into the flour mixture and bring together into a soft dough using a fork. If there are still dry crumbs, add a little more of the liquid. Turn out onto a lightly floured surface and knead briefly until smooth. Work in a little more flour if the mixture is sticky. Gently pat or roll out the dough to about 1 inch thick and cut out rounds using the cookie cutter, pressing the trimmings together to make more scones.

Arrange the scones on a greased baking sheet, spacing them slightly apart, and glaze the tops with the reserved egg and milk mixture. Bake for about 8 minutes, or until risen and golden. Transfer to a wire rack to cool slightly. Serve warm with clotted cream and strawberry jam.

These fruity, spiced, spiralled buns have been a traditional English treat since the eighteenth century. They were first made and sold by the celebrated Chelsea Bun House in Chelsea, west London.

baby chelsea buns

3½ cups white bread flour

1 teaspoon salt

¼ cup granulated sugar

a ¼-oz package of easy-blend dry yeast

6 tablespoons butter, melted

⅔ cup milk

2 eggs, beaten

⅓ cup packed soft brown sugar

1 teaspoon ground cinnamon

½ cup golden raisins

3 tablespoons currants

¼ cup dried apricots, chopped

honey, to glaze

an 8-inch square cake pan, greased

makes 16 buns

Sift the flour, salt, granulated sugar, and yeast in a large bowl and make a well in the center. Put 4 tablespoons of the butter in a small saucepan with the milk and heat until lukewarm. Remove from the heat, stir in the beaten eggs, then pour into the flour mixture, gradually working it in to make a soft dough. Turn out onto a lightly floured surface and knead for 5–10 minutes until smooth and elastic. Return to the bowl, wrap in a plastic bag, and let rise in a warm place for about 1 hour, or until doubled in size.

Punch down the dough, then divide into 4 equal pieces. Roll out each piece on a lightly floured surface to 5 x 8 inches. Combine the brown sugar, cinnamon, and dried fruits in a bowl and toss to mix. Pour the remaining melted butter over the dough, brushing it toward the edges to cover evenly. Sprinkle the fruit mixture on top and roll up tightly from the long edge to make 4 rolls.

Slice each roll into 4 whirls and arrange them in the prepared cake pan so that they are barely touching. Wrap in a plastic bag and let rise in a warm place for about 30 minutes, or until doubled in size.

Preheat the oven to 400°F.

Take the cake pan out of the plastic bag and bake for 20 minutes, or until golden. Glaze the buns with honey and bake for a further 5 minutes. Let cool in the pan for about 10 minutes, then turn out onto a wire rack and let cool completely. Pull the buns apart to serve.

3 cups all-purpose flour

⅓ cup stone-ground whole-wheat bread flour

¼ cup sugar

1 teaspoon sea salt

1 teaspoon apple pie spice

½ teaspoon freshly grated nutmeg

4 tablespoons unsalted butter, cubed

⅔ cup currants

⅓ cup golden raisins

¼ cup chopped mixed peel

a 0.6-oz cake compressed yeast

1¼ cups tepid milk

1 large egg, beaten

pastry cross

⅓ cup all-purpose flour

1½ tablespoons unsalted butter, cubed

2 teaspoons sugar

¼ cup milk mixed with 3 tablespoons sugar, to glaze

2 baking sheets, greased

makes 12 buns

Traditionally marked with a cross, these rich spicy fruit buns are eaten on Good Friday.

extra spicy hot cross buns

Put the flours, sugar, salt, and spices in a large bowl and mix well. Add the butter and rub into the flour using your fingertips until the mixture resembles fine crumbs. Mix in the dried fruit and mixed peel, then make a well in the center of the mixture.

Crumble the yeast into a small bowl, pour in about half the milk, and stir until completely dispersed. Add to the well in the flour with the rest of the milk and the egg. Gradually draw in the flour to make a soft but not sticky dough. Work in a little extra flour or milk if necessary.

Turn out the dough onto a lightly floured work surface and knead for 10 minutes. Return the dough to the bowl, then cover with plastic wrap. Let rise in a warm place until doubled in size, about 1½ hours.

Turn the dough out onto a lightly floured work surface, then punch down. Divide into 12 neat balls and set well apart on the prepared baking sheets. Slip the sheets into large plastic bags, inflate slightly, and let rise as before until doubled in size, 45–60 minutes. Meanwhile, preheat the oven to 400°F.

To make the pastry cross, put the flour, butter, and sugar in a bowl and rub the butter into the flour with your fingertips until you get coarse crumbs. Stir in 1–2 tablespoons cold water to make a firm dough. Roll the dough out thinly.

Uncover the risen buns, brush the pastry strips with a little water, then stick in a cross on top of the buns. Bake for 15–20 minutes, or until golden brown. Heat the milk-sugar glaze in a pan until dissolved, then boil for 1 minute. Glaze the buns as soon as they come out of the oven.

Rich and sweetly spiced, this teabread is known as Bara Brith in Wales, a name which means "speckled bread." It was traditionally made with leftover dough at the end of the day when the cook "speckled" the dough with currants. Mixed spice is often called pudding spice or sweet spice and reflects the centuries-long British love of spices.

welsh teabread

1¾ cups mixed dried fruit, such as raisins, currants, and citrus peel

1¼ cups hot black tea

2¼ cups all-purpose flour

2 teaspoons baking powder

1¼–1½ teaspoons mixed spice

1 stick unsalted butter, melted

¾ cup sugar or light brown sugar

½–1 teaspoon molasses, to color

1 egg, beaten

a 2-lb loaf pan, lined with parchment paper

makes 1 large teabread

Put the dried fruit in a bowl, add the hot tea, and let soak for at least 30 minutes. Drain the fruit and reserve the tea.

Preheat the oven to 325°F.

Put the flour, baking powder, and mixed spice in a bowl and mix well. Put the melted butter into a separate bowl, add the reserved tea, sugar, and molasses and mix well. Add the beaten egg and fruit and mix again.

Pour the fruit mixture gradually into the flour and mix well into a sloppy dough. Pour the dough into the prepared loaf pan and bake on the middle shelf of the oven for about 1 hour 15 minutes, or until a skewer inserted into the center comes out clean and the top is evenly brown. It should be dark and moist—be careful toward the end of baking as the top can scorch easily.

Remove from the oven and transfer to a wire rack. Let cool a little before serving. Cut thick slices, spread them with butter, then serve with a cup of tea—a perfect afternoon interlude.

2 sticks unsalted butter, at room temperature

2 cups plus 2 tablespoons sugar

4 large eggs, at room temperature, lightly beaten

1 teaspoon vanilla essence

1⅔ cups self-rising flour

3 oz bittersweet chocolate, chopped

1 tablespoon cocoa powder

3 oz white chocolate, chopped

a 2-lb loaf pan, greased and base-lined with parchment paper

makes 1 large loaf cake

The classic pound cake recipe uses equal weights of butter, flour, sugar, and eggs. It's very easy to turn the basic sponge mixture into an impressive, richly flavored marbled loaf. Serve thick slices with a cup of tea or coffee and watch the cake disappear in no time.

black and white chocolate marble loaf cake

Preheat the oven to 350°F.

Put the butter into a large mixing bowl and beat until very creamy. Beat in the sugar and continue beating for about 2 minutes, or until the mixture is lighter in color and consistency. Gradually beat in the eggs, then the vanilla essence. Sift in the flour and fold in with a metal spoon.

Spoon half the cake mixture into another mixing bowl. Put the bittersweet chocolate in a heatproof bowl set over a pan of simmering water and melt gently (do not let the base of the bowl touch the water). Remove from the heat and let cool. Sift the cocoa onto one portion of cake mixture, add the bittersweet chocolate, then, using a metal spoon, fold in until evenly mixed.

Melt the white chocolate as above. When cool, fold into the remaining portion of cake mixture using a clean metal spoon.

Spoon both cake mixtures into the prepared pan, using each mixture alternately. Draw a knife through the mixtures and swirl together.

Bake for about 1¼ hours, or until a skewer inserted in the center comes out clean. Turn out onto a wire rack, remove the lining and let cool.

Named after Queen Victoria, this classic cake filled with cream and fresh fruit makes a wonderful centerpiece for a traditional afternoon tea. Make it in summer when strawberries are in season and at their best.

victoria sponge cake
with strawberries and cream

1½ sticks butter, at room temperature

¾ cup plus 2 tablespoons sugar

3 eggs

1½ cups self-rising flour

3½ tablespoons good-quality strawberry jam

1 cup strawberries, hulled and halved or quartered, depending on size

½ cup whipping cream

confectioners' sugar, to dust

two 8-inch cake pans, greased and base-lined with parchment paper

serves 6–8

Preheat the oven to 350°F.

Beat together the butter and sugar in a large bowl until pale and fluffy. Beat in the eggs one at a time. Sift the flour into the mixture and fold in until thoroughly combined.

Spoon the cake mixture into the prepared pans and spread out evenly using the back of the spoon. Bake for 20–25 minutes, or until golden brown and the sponge springs back when pressed gently with the tips of your fingers. Turn out the cakes onto a wire rack, gently peel off the lining paper, and let cool completely.

To serve, slice a thin slither off the top of one of the cakes to create a flat surface. Spread the strawberry jam on top and top with the strawberries. Whip the cream until it stands in soft peaks, then spread on top of the strawberries. Top with the second cake, press down gently and dust with confectioners' sugar.

Picture a traditional afternoon tea at an English tea parlor and there is bound to be a luscious coffee cake topped with crisp brown walnuts. An old favorite that never fails to please.

coffee and walnut cake

1½ sticks butter, at room temperature

¾ cup plus 2 tablespoons sugar

3 eggs

1½ cups self-rising flour

⅓ cup walnut pieces

2 teaspoons instant coffee, dissolved in 1 tablespoon boiling water

walnut halves, to decorate

frosting

2 tablespoons light cream

2 teaspoons instant coffee

6 tablespoons butter, at room temperature

1 scant cup confectioners' sugar

two 8-inch cake pans, greased and base-lined with parchment paper

serves 6–8

Preheat the oven to 350°F.

Beat together the butter and sugar in a large bowl until pale and fluffy, then beat in the eggs one at a time. Sift the flour into the butter mixture and fold in, then fold in the nuts and dissolved coffee. Divide among the prepared cake pans and spread out evenly. Bake for 20–25 minutes, or until golden and the sponge springs back when pressed gently with the tips of your fingers. Turn the cakes out onto a wire rack, carefully peel off the lining paper, and let cool completely.

To make the frosting, warm the cream and coffee in a small saucepan, stirring until the coffee has dissolved. Pour into a bowl, add the butter, and sift the confectioners' sugar into the mixture. Beat together until smooth and creamy.

To serve, slice a thin slither off the top of one of the cakes to create a flat surface. Spread with slightly less than half of the frosting, then place the second cake on top. Spread the remaining frosting on top and decorate with walnut halves.

3 cups self-rising flour

⅔ cup cocoa powder

a good pinch of salt

2 cups sugar

1 cup sunflower oil

2 large eggs, beaten

1 cup milk

1 teaspoon vanilla essence

1 cup semisweet chocolate chips

frosting

1 stick unsalted butter, softened

2¾ cups confectioners' sugar

6 tablespoons cocoa powder

¼ cup milk

½ teaspoon vanilla essence

three 8-inch cake pans

serves 8

If you can make muffins, you can make this cake. It is really a rich chocolate chip muffin recipe, so just measure and mix. The frosting is a simple butter frosting made with cocoa.

triple chocolate layer cake

Preheat the oven to 350°F. Grease the cake pans and base-line with parchment paper.

Sift the flour, cocoa, salt, and sugar into a large bowl, and make a well in the center. Pour the oil, beaten eggs, milk, and vanilla essence into the well, and mix gradually with a wooden spoon. Add the chocolate chips and stir well. Divide the mixture between the 3 prepared cake pans.

Bake for 20–25 minutes, or until a skewer inserted in the center comes out clean. Let cool in the tins for 5 minutes, then carefully turn out onto a wire rack to cool completely.

To make the frosting, put the butter in a bowl and beat until very creamy. Gradually beat in the confectioners' sugar, cocoa, milk, and vanilla essence to make a thick, smooth frosting.

When the cakes are completely cold, use the frosting to layer them. Spread about one-sixth of the frosting on the top of one cake. Gently set a second cake on top and spread with another one-sixth of the frosting. Top with the last cake, then coat the top and sides with the rest of the frosting. Decorate with extra chopped chocolate, if desired.

Make this sensational summer drink when lemons are ripe and plentiful. Leave the lemons on a warm windowsill for a few days to sweeten them up and develop their flavor. You can make this a day or two ahead. It must be served as cold as possible.

real old-fashioned lemonade

Using a potato peeler, remove the yellow peel from the lemons in long strips, avoiding any bitter white pith. Put it in a large heatproof pitcher, add the sugar, and pour over the boiling water. Stir well to dissolve the sugar, cover, and let cool completely.

Squeeze the juice from the lemons, strain, and set aside. When the lemon-scented water is cold, stir in the lemon juice and strain into a pitcher. Chill well and serve poured over ice, with a sprig of mint or lemon balm, if using.

3 unwaxed lemons, scrubbed in warm water

1 cup sugar

1 quart boiling water

sprigs of mint or lemon balm (optional)

serves 2–4

In Victorian times, kitchen maids would boil up the lemon and barley, strain it through cheesecloth, let it cool, then struggle to find a way to chill it. Thank goodness for ice!

lemon barley water

Put the barley and water in a saucepan and simmer for 30 minutes. Strain into a cafetière, then stir in the sugar, lemon peel, and juice. Let cool, plunge, chill, then serve over ice with a curl of lemon peel.

2 tablespoons pearl barley

1.5 quarts boiling water

grated peel and juice of 1 large unwaxed lemon

2 teaspoons sugar

a curl of lemon peel

ice, to serve

serves 2–4

preserves

Chutney, a cherished sweet and spicy condiment on the British table, is an Anglo-Indian remnant from the days of the East India Company and the Raj. Homemade versions have always been popular in England—an aspect of the national taste for jams and pickles to serve with bread, cheese, and cold meats. They have acquired a distinctively British flavor, different from their originals in India.

plum chutney

1¾ lb plums, about 14, pitted and chopped

1⅓ cups raisins

1 large onion, chopped

½ teaspoon salt

⅔ cup cider vinegar

1½ teaspoons coriander seeds, 1 teaspoon allspice berries, 10 cloves, ¼ teaspoon black peppercorns and ¾ teaspoon mustard seeds, all in a spice ball or tied up in cheesecloth

½ teaspoon ground ginger

a good pinch of freshly grated nutmeg

¾ cup sugar or light brown sugar

two sterilized 2-cup jars with non-metal lids (see page 4)

two wax disks

makes about 1 quart chutney

Put the plums, raisins, onion, and salt into a stainless steel (not copper) preserving pan or heavy-based saucepan and add the vinegar. Stir, then add the ball or bag of pickling spices. Bring to a boil, reduce the heat, and simmer gently for about 40 minutes, stirring occasionally. Be careful not to scorch the chutney as it cooks and thickens.

Add the ginger, nutmeg, and sugar and mix well. Keep a close eye on the chutney and cook for another 10–15 minutes, stirring regularly to make sure it doesn't burn. It should be dark and tangy yet sweet and thick. As it cools and sets, it will become thicker still.

Remove the ball or bag of pickling spices and pour the chutney into the sterilized jars while still hot. Line the lids with wax disks and seal at once.

There are many varieties of pumpkin and this recipe can be used to preserve all of them. Make sure that the flesh is firm and not stringy, or it will spoil the finished texture of the chutney. You can also use other vegetables such as squash, zucchini, eggplant, unripe melons, and green tomatoes to make this recipe. Serve with bread and cheese, scrambled eggs, or cold cuts.

pumpkin and red tomato chutney

1 lb peeled and seeded firm pumpkin or butternut squash flesh, cut into ½-inch cubes

1 large ripe tomato, peeled, seeded, and chopped

1 large onion, chopped

⅔ cup golden raisins

1¼ cups soft brown sugar

1 teaspoon salt

1 inch fresh ginger, peeled and finely chopped

1 garlic clove, peeled and finely chopped

a little freshly grated nutmeg

1 cup malt vinegar, plus ½ cup extra

a sterilized 1-pint jar with lid or cover (see page 4)

a wax paper disk

makes 1 pint chutney

Put the pumpkin, tomatoes, onions, golden raisins, sugar, salt, ginger, garlic, nutmeg, and the 1 cup vinegar in a saucepan and bring slowly to a boil. Simmer for 1 hour, stirring from time to time. The chutney should look dark, dense, and rich. Top up with extra vinegar if the chutney dries out too much while cooking.

Transfer to the sterilized jar, cover the surface of the chutney with a wax paper disk, and seal at once. Label when cool and store for 1–6 months in a cool, dark pantry before opening.

Like the Pumpkin and Red Tomato Chutney on page 224, these pickled onions are perfect with slices of crusty bread and some flavorful cheese.

pickled onions

3 tablespoons salt

1 lb shallots or pickling onions, such as pearl onions

spiced vinegar

8 mixed peppercorns

4 whole cloves

½ inch cinnamon stick

½ inch fresh ginger

1¾ cups malt vinegar

a sterilized 1-pint jar with lid (see page 4)

a wax paper disk

makes 1 pint pickled onions

Put the salt in a saucepan with 2¾ cups water. Bring to a boil, remove from the heat, and let cool.

Put the shallots in a large bowl, pour boiling water over them, and leave for a few minutes. Drain and peel.

Put the shallots in a bowl, add the cooled brine, and leave for 24 hours. After this time, drain, rinse in cold water and dry carefully.

To make the spiced vinegar, put the peppercorns, cloves, cinnamon, and ginger in a small saucepan, add the vinegar, cover, and bring to a boil over low heat. Turn off the heat, let cool, then strain.

Pack the onions into the sterilized jar, pushing them down with the handle of a wooden spoon. Top up with the cooled spiced vinegar.

Tap the sides to remove any air bubbles or slide a thin knife blade down the inside of the jar to release them.

Cover with a waxed paper disk, seal the jar, and store in a cool, dark pantry until required. Wait at least 3 months before serving.

Marmalade epitomizes an English breakfast. The beauty of this particular marmalade is that it can be made in small quantities at any time of the year, not just when Sevilles are in season.

chunky lemon, lime, and grapefruit marmalade

1 unwaxed lemon

1 small unwaxed pink grapefruit

1 unwaxed lime

5 cups sugar

freshly squeezed juice of ½ lemon

three ½-pint sterilized jam jars with lids or covers (see page 4)

wax paper disks

makes about 1½ pints marmalade

Scrub the fruit and prise out any stalk ends. Put in a pan and cover with 2 cups water. Set over low heat and cook until tender—1½–2 hours. The fruit is ready when it "collapses."

Transfer the fruit to a cutting board and leave until cool enough to handle. Cut in half, scrape out all the flesh and seeds, and add to the pan of water. Bring to a boil and simmer for 5 minutes. Cut the peel into strips, or put it in a blender and blend until chunky. Strain the water from the seeds and flesh and return it to the pan, adding the chopped peel and the lemon juice. Discard the seeds and debris.

Add the sugar to the pan and bring slowly to simmering point, stirring until the sugar has dissolved. The sugar content is high, so this will take quite a long time. When the marmalade has become translucent, you will know the sugar has dissolved and you can increase the heat. Bring to a boil and boil rapidly until setting point is reached—5–10 minutes.

Take the pan off the heat and test for set (see page 4). If the marmalade is not ready, put the pan back on the heat to boil for a few more minutes and test again. When setting point has been reached, return to simmering point, then turn off the heat. Skim with a perforated skimmer, stir well, and let stand for 30 minutes. Stir and ladle into the sterilized jars, seal with wax paper disks, and cover with a lid. Let cool, label, and store in a cool, dark pantry until needed.

Strawberry and raspberry jam—delicious on scones, crumpets, and toast—but super easy and quick to make.

strawberry jam

1 lb fresh ripe strawberries, hulled and quartered

1¾ cups sugar with added pectin (sometimes known as "jam sugar")

two 1-pint sterilized jam jars with lids or covers (see page 4)

makes 1½ pots, 1 pint each

Put the strawberries in a large bowl with a splash of water. Cover and microwave on FULL for 2 minutes. Carefully uncover and stir in the sugar. Re-cover and cook on FULL for another 2 minutes.

Uncover and stir well to dissolve the sugar. Replace in the microwave uncovered and cook on FULL for 8 minutes.

Test by dropping a teaspoon onto a chilled saucer and chilling in the refrigerator for 10 minutes. If it has set, pour the jam into clean dry jars and cover. If not, microwave for 4 more minutes, then try the test again. Pour into the sterilized jars and seal. After opening, the jam will keep in the refrigerator for up to 2 weeks.

freezer raspberry jam

1½ lb fresh raspberries

5 cups sugar with added pectin (sometimes known as "jam sugar")

2 tablespoons freshly squeezed lemon juice

two 1-pint sterilized jam jars with lids or covers (see page 4)

makes 2 pots, 1 pint each

Tip the raspberries into a bowl and crush a bit with a potato masher. Stir in the jam sugar and lemon juice. Cover with plastic wrap and heat on MEDIUM in the microwave for about 5 minutes or until warmed through.

Uncover and stir gently to dissolve the sugar, then let stand overnight. Alternatively, heat in a saucepan until the sugar has dissolved.

The next day, pot up into freezer containers and freeze—keep one pot in the refrigerator for breakfast tomorrow. After removing from the freezer, store the jam in the refrigerator. Thaw before using.

If you have space for a small tree in your garden, it's worth planting a crabapple. You will have pretty blossom in spring and jewel-like miniature apples in the late summer to early fall. Use them to make this stunning pink jelly to serve with roast pork, poultry, and game.

crabapple jelly

3 lb crabapples

1 unwaxed lemon

sugar

a jelly bag or muslin

two or three sterilized ½-pint jam jars with lids or covers (see page 4)

wax paper disks

makes 1–1½ pints jelly

Sort the crabapples, discarding any that are badly bruised or marked and any leaves that are still attached. Wash the fruit, cut them in half, and put in a large saucepan. Fill the pan with water to just under the level of the fruit. Thinly grate the peel from the lemon and add this and the peeled lemon to the pan. Part-cover with a lid, bring slowly to a boil, and simmer for 1 hour. Transfer to a jelly bag or cheesecloth suspended over a large bowl and leave to drip all night.

Measure the juice into a clean preserving pan and, for every 2½ cups juice, add 2¼ cups sugar. Set over low heat and bring to simmering point, dissolving the sugar, stirring all the while. When it has dissolved, increase the heat and boil hard for 5–10 minutes, or until setting point is reached.

Take the pan off the heat and test for set (see page 4). If the jelly is not ready, put the pan back on the heat to boil for a few more minutes and test again. When setting point has been reached, return to simmering point, then turn off the heat. Skim with a perforated skimmer, stir and ladle into the sterilized jars. Seal with wax paper disks and cover with a lid. Let cool, label, and store in a cool, dark pantry until needed.

This is a quintessentially British preserve, tart with lemon yet sweet and buttery at the same time. It is delicious on toast or on freshly made scones or bread and also an excellent filling for tarts, sponge cakes, or meringues. Small jars make a great gift. It is very easy to make so long as you stir it very frequently as it cooks and keep the heat low so that the water in the pan barely bubbles.

lemon curd

2 large unwaxed lemons

1 stick unsalted butter, cubed

1 cup sugar

3 eggs, beaten

two 8-oz sterilized jam jars with lids or covers (see page 4)

**makes 2 small jars,
8 oz each**

Finely grate the peel from the lemons into a heatproof bowl. Squeeze the juice and add that to the bowl with the butter and sugar.

Place the bowl over a pan of just-simmering water, making sure the water doesn't touch the base of the bowl. Stir until the butter melts, add the eggs, and, using a wooden spoon, stir for 10–15 minutes until the mixture thickens noticeably and takes on a translucent look.

For a very smooth preserve, strain the curd through a fine-meshed strainer into a measuring jug, then pot it into the sterilized jars. Cover with plastic wrap or waxed paper when cold. It will keep for 15 days in the refrigerator.

index

A

almonds: little Richmond maids of honor 186

old English trifle 161

rhubarb and orange crumble 144

traditional Christmas pudding 163

anchovies: little toasts with anchovy butter 183

marinated roast venison 66

apples: baked stuffed apples with butterscotch sauce 137

classic apple pie 155

classic blackberry and apple crumble 140

crabapple jelly 232

mini pork and apple pies 88

pork steaks with apple and blackberry compote 93

roast apples and celery root or parsnips 118

roast goose 65

rolled pork roast with sage and onion stuffing 96

traditional Christmas pudding 163

asparagus: green vegetable salad with hazelnut dressing 28

B

bacon: beef and mushroom pies 86

chestnut stuffing 106

cottage pie 105

fresh pea soup with mint and crispy bacon 17

loin of pork with a herb crust 94

mini pork and apple pies 88

roast chicken with lemon, thyme, and potato stuffing 60

roast rabbit with herbs and cider 69

sausage and bacon toad-in-the-hole 91

Savoy cabbage with bacon and cream 121

beef: beef and carrot casserole with cheesy dumplings 79

beef and mushroom pies 86

beef Wellington 83

cock-a-leekie 59

cottage pie 105

Irish carbonnade 80

rare beef salad with watercress 31

roast beef with all the trimmings 74

steak and kidney pudding 85

Stilton steaks with sweet potato and garlic mash 76

beets, roast 117

black and white chocolate marble loaf cake 210

blackberries: blackberry cranachan 139

classic blackberry and apple crumble 140

pork steaks with apple and blackberry compote 93

bread 169–78

bread and butter puddings 129

little toasts with anchovy butter 183

loin of pork with a herb crust 94

summer pudding 131

Welsh rabbit 18

bread sauce 106

butterscotch sauce 164

C

cabbage: Savoy cabbage with bacon and cream 121

Caerphilly and leek bread 175

cakes: black and white chocolate

marble loaf cake 210

coffee and walnut cake 215

triple layer chocolate cake 216

Victoria sponge cake with strawberries and cream 212

carrots: beef and carrot casserole with cheesy dumplings 79

beef and mushroom pies 86

lamb shanks with red wine, rosemary, and garlic 100

Lancashire hotpot 102

roast rabbit with herbs and cider 69

celery root: roast apples and celery root or parsnips 118

smoked haddock stew with potatoes and celery root 42

champ 114

cheese: baby cheese scones 184

beef and carrot casserole with cheesy dumplings 79

champ 114

cheese and leek bread 175

cottage pie 105

little Richmond maids of honor 186

mashed potatoes 112

Stilton steaks 76

sweet pear and Stilton melt 23

Welsh rabbit 18

Yorkshire cheesecake 152

cheesecake, Yorkshire 152

Chelsea buns, baby 205

chestnut stuffing 106

chicken: cock-a-leekie 59

roast chicken with lemon, thyme, and potato stuffing 60

chicken livers: chicken liver salad 32

mini pork and apple pies 88

chocolate: black and white chocolate marble loaf cake 210

triple layer chocolate cake 216

white and black desserts 148

Christmas pudding 163

cock-a-leekie 59

cod: fish supper 54

roast cod with mustard mash 47

coffee and walnut cake 215

cottage pie 105

crabapple jelly 232

cranberries: baked stuffed apples with butterscotch sauce 137

cranberry and raspberry jellies 156

cranberry relish 107

sweet pear and Stilton melt 23

cranberry juice: cranberry and raspberry jellies 156

cream: blackberry cranachan 139

bread and butter puddings 129

butterscotch sauce 164

horseradish sauce 125

old English trifle 161

orange syllabub with crunchy orange sprinkle 158

plum fudge desserts 147

Savoy cabbage with bacon and cream 121

scones with clotted cream and strawberry jam 203

smoked haddock stew with potatoes and celery root 42

sticky toffee pudding 150

Victoria sponge cake with strawberries and cream 212

white and black desserts 148

Yorkshire cheesecake 152

crème fraiche: broiled rainbow trout fillets with mustard and caper butter 48

cream of mushroom soup 14

leek and potato soup with watercress purée 12

crumpets 198
custard, real English 164

D
dates: sticky toffee pudding 150

E
easy fish stew 40
Easter cookies 192
eggs: baby cheese scones 184
  baby Chelsea buns 205
  black and white chocolate marble loaf cake 210
  bread and butter puddings 129
  coffee and walnut cake 215
  Easter cookies 192
  kedgeree 39
  lemon curd 234
  little nutmeg and bay leaf custard tarts 189
  little Richmond maids of honor 186
  old English trifle 161
  real English custard 164
  sticky toffee pudding 150
  traditional Christmas pudding 163
  triple layer chocolate cake 216
  Victoria sponge cake with strawberries and cream 212
  Welsh teabread 209
  white and black desserts 148
  Yorkshire cheesecake 152
  Yorkshire puddings and horseradish sauce 125
English custard 164

F
fava beans: smoked salmon salad 26
fish 37–54

fruit, dried: toasted teacakes 200
  Welsh teabread 209
  see also currants; raisins *etc.*
fruit: summer pudding 131
  see also apples; pears *etc.*

G
game 66–71
goose: roast goose 65
gooseberry and ginger wine crumble 142
grapefruit: chunky lemon, lime, and grapefruit marmalade 228
gravy 107
green beans: green vegetable salad with hazelnut dressing 28
  roast guinea fowl with new potatoes and green beans 71
guinea fowl: roast guinea fowl with new potatoes and green beans 71

H
haddock: fish supper 54
  kedgeree 39
  smoked haddock stew with potatoes and celery root 42
  traditional fish pie 37
halibut: crisp-fried herbed halibut with shoestring potatoes 44
hazelnuts: green vegetable salad with hazelnut dressing 28
  roast cod with mustard mash 47
  sweet pear and Stilton melt 23
horseradish sauce 125
hot cross buns, extra spicy 206

I
Irish carbonnade 80

J
jam: chunky lemon, lime, and

grapefruit marmalade 228
crabapple jelly 232
old English trifle 161
scones with clotted cream and strawberry jam 203
freezer raspberry jam 231
strawberry jam
Victoria sponge cake with strawberries and cream 212
jellies, cranberry and raspberry 156

K
kedgeree 39
kidneys: steak and kidney pudding 85

L
lamb: lamb shanks with red wine, rosemary, and garlic 100
  Lancashire hotpot 102
  pot roast leg of lamb with rosemary and onion gravy 99
Lancashire hotpot 102
leeks: cheese and leek bread 175
  cock-a-leekie 59
  easy fish stew 40
  Lancashire hotpot 102
  leek and potato soup with watercress purée 12
  watercress soup 11
lemonade, real old-fashioned 219
lemons: chunky lemon, lime, and grapefruit marmalade 228
  crabapple jelly 232
  Easter cookies 192
  lemon curd 234
  little Richmond maids of honor 186
  pears in port with juniper and ginger 134
  real old-fashioned lemonade

219
  roast chicken with lemon, thyme, and potato stuffing 60
  salmon baked in newspaper 51
  traditional Christmas pudding 163
  wilted greens 122
  Yorkshire cheesecake 152

M
marmalade, chunky lemon, lime, and grapefruit 228
meat 74–106
mincemeat pies 190
monkfish: easy fish stew 40
mushrooms: beef and mushroom pies 86
  beef Wellington 83
  cream of mushroom soup 14
  mussels: easy fish stew 40

O
oatmeal: oatcakes 178
  parkin cookies 195
onions: beef and carrot casserole with cheesy dumplings 79
  cock-a-leekie 59
  cottage pie 105
  easy fish stew 40

Irish carbonnade 80
Lancashire hotpot 102
pickled onions 226
plum chutney 223
pumpkin and red tomato chutney 224
roast chicken with lemon, thyme, and potato stuffing 60
rolled pork roast with sage and onion stuffing 96
oranges: orange syllabub with crunchy orange sprinkle 158
rhubarb and orange crumble 144

P
parkin cookies 195
parsley: char-grilled scallops with parsley oil 25
cock-a-leekie 59
cottage pie 105
cream of mushroom soup 14
crisp-fried herbed halibut with shoestring potatoes 44
easy fish stew 40
loin of pork with a herb crust 94
roast apples and celery root or parsnips 118
roast cod with mustard mash 47

smoked haddock stew with potatoes and celery root 42
traditional fish cakes 52
parsnips: roast apples and celery root or parsnips 118
roast beef with all the trimmings 74
peaches: old English trifle 161
pearl barley: cock-a-leekie 59
pears: pears in port with juniper and ginger 134
sweet pear and Stilton melt 23
peas: broiled rainbow trout fillets with mustard and caper butter 48
fresh pea soup with mint and crispy bacon 17
green vegetable salad with hazelnut dressing 28
pickled onions 226
pies: beef and mushroom pies 86
classic apple pie 155
mincemeat pies 190
mini pork and apple pies 88
plums: plum chutney 223
plum fudge desserts 147
pork: loin of pork with a herb crust 94
mini pork and apple pies 88
pork steaks with apple and blackberry compote 93
rolled pork roast with sage and onion stuffing 96
port: pears in port with juniper and ginger 134
potatoes: broiled rainbow trout fillets with mustard and caper butter 48
champ 114
cock-a-leekie 59
cottage pie 105
crisp-fried herbed halibut with shoestring potatoes 44

fish supper 54
Lancashire hotpot 102
leek and potato soup with watercress purée 12
mashed potatoes 112
potato bread rolls 177
roast beef with all the trimmings 74
roast chicken with lemon, thyme, and potato stuffing 60
roast guinea fowl with new potatoes and green beans 71
roast potatoes 111
roast cod with mustard mash 47
smoked haddock stew with potatoes and celery root 42
smoked salmon salad 26
traditional fish cakes 52
traditional fish pie 37
watercress soup 11
potatoes, sweet: Stilton steaks with sweet potato and garlic mash 76
poultry and game 59–71
preserves 223–34
prunes: cock-a-leekie 59
roast goose 65
pumpkin and red tomato chutney 224

Q
quails' eggs: little toasts with anchovy butter 183

R
rabbit: roast rabbit with herbs and cider 69
rainbow trout fillets, broiled, with mustard and caper butter 48
raisins: baked stuffed apples with butterscotch sauce 137
plum chutney 223
raisin and rosemary bread 172

traditional Christmas pudding 163
Yorkshire cheesecake 152
raspberries: cranberry and raspberry jellies 156
freezer raspberry jam 231
red wine: beef and carrot casserole with cheesy dumplings 79
beef and mushroom pies 86
chicken liver salad 32
lamb shanks with red wine, rosemary, and garlic 100
loin of pork with a herb crust 94
pears in port with juniper and ginger 134
summer pudding 131
wine gravy 107
rhubarb and orange crumble 144
rice: kedgeree 39
rice pudding 132

S
salads: chicken liver salad 32
green vegetable salad with hazelnut dressing 28
rare beef salad with watercress 31
smoked salmon salad 26
salmon: salmon baked in newspaper 51
smoked salmon salad 26
sauces: bread sauce 106
butterscotch sauce 164
horseradish sauce 125
sausage and bacon toad-in-the-hole 91
sausage meat: chestnut stuffing 106
roast chicken with lemon, thyme, and potato stuffing 60
sausage rolls 20

Savoy cabbage with bacon and cream 121

scallops: char-grilled scallops with parsley oil 25

easy fish stew 40

scones: baby cheese scones 184

scones with clotted cream and strawberry jam 203

Scottish shortbread 196

seafood see cod; mussels etc.

shellfish see mussels.; shrimp etc.

shrimp: easy fish stew 40

side dishes 111–25

soda bread 170

soups: cream of mushroom soup 14

fresh pea soup with mint and crispy bacon 17

leek and potato soup with watercress purée 12

watercress soup 11

steak and kidney pudding 85

sticky toffee pudding 150

Stilton steaks with sweet potato and garlic mash 76

strawberries: strawberry jam 231

Victoria sponge cake with strawberries and cream 212

stuffing 60

chestnut stuffing 106

summer pudding 131

sweet pear and Stilton melt 23

sweet potatoes: Stilton steaks with sweet potato and garlic mash 76

T

tarts: little nutmeg and bay leaf custard tarts 189

little Richmond maids of honor 186

tea: Welsh teabread 209

teacakes, toasted 200

toasted teacakes 200

tomatoes: easy fish stew 40

pumpkin and red tomato chutney 224

treacle: Welsh teabread 209

trifle, old English 161

triple layer chocolate cake 216

trout: broiled rainbow trout fillets with mustard and caper butter 48

turkey: traditional roast turkey 62

V

vegetables: green vegetable salad with hazelnut dressing 28

wilted greens 122

see also leeks; peas etc.

venison: marinated roast venison 66

Victoria sponge cake with strawberries and cream 212

W

walnuts: coffee and walnut cake 215

Welsh rabbit 18

Welsh teabread 209

white and black desserts 148

white wine: cottage pie 105

orange syllabub with crunchy orange sprinkle 158

pot roast leg of lamb with rosemary and onion gravy 99

wilted greens 122

wine see red wine; white wine

wine gravy 107

Y, Z

Yorkshire cheesecake 152

Yorkshire puddings and horseradish sauce 125

zucchini: green vegetable salad with hazelnut dressing 28

conversion charts

Weights and measures have been rounded up or down slightly to make measuring easier.

Volume equivalents

American	Metric	Imperial
1 teaspoon	5 ml	
1 tablespoon	15 ml	
$\frac{1}{4}$ cup	60 ml	2 fl.oz.
$\frac{1}{3}$ cup	75 ml	$2\frac{1}{2}$ fl.oz.
$\frac{1}{2}$ cup	125 ml	4 fl.oz.
$\frac{2}{3}$ cup	150 ml	5 fl.oz. ($\frac{1}{4}$ pint)
$\frac{3}{4}$ cup	175 ml	6 fl.oz.
1 cup	250 ml	8 fl.oz.

Weight equivalents

Imperial	Metric
1 oz.	25 g
2 oz.	50 g
3 oz.	75 g
4 oz.	125 g
5 oz.	150 g
6 oz.	175 g
7 oz.	200 g
8 oz. ($\frac{1}{2}$ lb.)	250 g
9 oz.	275 g
10 oz.	300 g
11 oz.	325 g
12 oz.	375 g
13 oz.	400 g
14 oz.	425 g
15 oz.	475 g
16 oz. (1 lb.)	500 g
2 1b.	1 kg

Measurements

Inches	cm
$\frac{1}{4}$ inch	5 mm
$\frac{1}{2}$ inch	1 cm
$\frac{3}{4}$ inch	1.5 cm
1 inch	2.5 cm
2 inches	5 cm
3 inches	7 cm
4 inches	10 cm
5 inches	12 cm
6 inches	15 cm
7 inches	18 cm
8 inches	20 cm
9 inches	23 cm
10 inches	25 cm
11 inches	28 cm
12 inches	30 cm

1 stick butter = 8 tablespoons = 125 g

Oven temperatures

225°F	110°C	Gas $\frac{1}{4}$
250°F	120°C	Gas $\frac{1}{2}$
275°F	140°C	Gas 1
300°F	150°C	Gas 2
325°F	160°C	Gas 3
350°F	180°C	Gas 4
375°F	190°C	Gas 5
400°F	200°C	Gas 6
425°F	220°C	Gas 7
450°F	230°C	Gas 8
475°F	240°C	Gas 9

recipe credits

Sonia Stevenson

Traditional fish pie
Irish carbonnade
Steak and kidney pudding
Traditional roast turkey
Roast goose
Marinated roast venison
Roast rabbit
Roast beef
Loin of pork
Rolled pork roast
Cranberry relish
Gravy
Wine gravy
Chestnut stuffing
Bread sauce
Roast apples and celery root
Yorkshire puddings
Horseradish sauce

Maxine Clark

Little nutmeg and bay leaf custard tarts
Leek and potato soup
Beef and mushroom pies
Pot roast leg of lamb
Real old-fashioned lemonade
Strawberry jam
Freezer raspberry jam
Yorkshire cheesecake
Little Richmond maids of honor
Salmon baked in newspaper
Classic blackberry and apple crumble
Gooseberry and ginger wine crumble
Rhubarb and orange crumble
Butterscotch sauce
Real English custard

Linda Collister

White and black desserts
Black and white marble loaf
Sticky toffee pudding
Old-fashioned cottage loaf
Cheese and leek bread
Potato bread rolls
Extra spicy hot cross buns
Triple chocolate layer cake
Oatcakes
Easter cookies
Parkin cookies
Scottish shortbread

Fran Warde

Traditional fish cakes
Roast chicken
Beef and carrot casserole
Sausage and bacon toad-in-the-hole
Lancashire hotpot
Roast potatoes
Watercress soup
Easy fish stew
Beef Wellington
Baked stuffed apples
Chicken liver salad

Susannah Blake

Little toasts with anchovy butter
Baby cheese scones
Toasted teacakes
Scones
Baby Chelsea buns
Victoria sponge
Coffee and walnut cake

Lindy Wildsmith

Pumpkin and red tomato chutney
Pickled onions
Chunky lemon, lime, and grapefruit marmalade
Crabapple jelly
Roast guinea fowl

Laura Washburn

Cottage pie
Rice pudding
Roast beets
Savoy cabbage with bacon and cream
Wilted greens

Louise Pickford

Pork steaks
Bread and butter puddings
Plum fudge desserts
Soda bread
Mini pork and apple pies

Rachael Anne Hill

Sweet pear and Stilton melt
Kedgeree
Stilton steaks
Summer pudding

Clare Ferguson

Char-grilled scallops
Mashed potatoes
Fish supper
Cock-a-leekie

Manisha Gambhir Harkins

Classic apple pie
Welsh teabread
Plum chutney

Fiona Beckett

Lamb shanks
Orange syllabub
Raisin and rosemary bread

Caroline Marson

Broiled rainbow trout fillets
Blackberry cranachan

Tessa Bramley

Smoked haddock stew
Pears in port

Linda Tubby

Crisp-fried herbed halibut

Kate Habershon

Crumpets

Annie Nichols

Champ

Celia Brooks Brown

Welsh rabbit

Clare Gordon-Smith

Roast cod with mustard mash

Brian Glover

Lemon curd

Tamsin Burnett-Hall

Cranberry and raspberry jellies

Anne Sheasby

Sausage rolls
Old English trifle
Traditional Christmas pudding
Mincemeat pies

Elsa Petersen-Schepelern

Smoked salmon salad
Green vegetable salad
Rare beef salad
Cream of mushroom soup
Fresh pea soup
Lemon barley water

photography credits

Martin Brigdale

Pages 6, 21, 56, 57, 63, 64, 67, 68, 70, 73r, 75, 95, 97, 98, 104, 106r, 107l, 107c, 111, 119, 124, 125, 127r, 133, 149, 153, 158, 160, 162, 166, 167 all, 168, 174, 176, 177, 181c, 181r, 182, 185, 187, 188, 191, 195, 201, 202, 204, 207, 210, 211, 212, 213, 214

Peter Cassidy

Pages 8, 9 all, 11, 15, 16, 24, 27, 29, 30, 35l, 44, 45, 49, 53, 58, 69, 92, 107r, 109c, 113, 114, 126, 128, 138, 140, 141, 142, 143, 144, 145, 146, 147, 154, 155, 165, 171, 189, 208, 221l, 222, 223, 237

William Lingwood

Pages 34, 35r, 36, 50, 81, 84, 101, 106l, 159, 199

William Reavell

Pages 35c, 76, 127l, 127c, 131, 157, 178

Nicki Dowey

Pages 22, 38, 77, 130, 205, 221c

Diana Miller

Pages 179, 180, 193, 194, 197, 217

David Munns

Pages 18, 23, 116, 120, 123, 173

Caroline Arber

Pages 61, 78, 90, 103, 110

Richard Jung

Pages 7, 60, 216, 221r, 235

Debi Treloar

Pages 10, 33, 41, 82, 136

Tara Fisher

Pages 225, 227, 229, 233

James Merrell

Endpapers, pages 46, 219, 226

Peter Myers

Pages 108, 109r, 115, 238

Noel Murphy

Pages 13, 87, 218, 230

Chris Tubbs

Page 1; 2 (Ros Byam Shaw's house in Devon); 3; 5

Henry Bourne

Pages 37, 59, 73c

Craig Robertson

Pages 43, 72, 135

Ian Wallace

Pages 73l, 89

Polly Wreford

Pages 109l, 151

David Brittain

Page 220

Jean Cazals

Page 181l

Jeremy Hopley

Page 55

Sandra Lane

Page 232

Philip Webb

Page 19

Alan Williams

Page 65